Cooking *with* Convection

ALSO BY BEATRICE OJAKANGAS

Beatrice Ojakangas

Cooking *with* Convection

Broadway Books

New York

PRINTED IN THE UNITED STATES OF AMERICA

BROADWAY BOOKS and its logo, a letter B bisected on the diagonal, are trademarks of Random House, Inc.

Visit our website at www.broadwaybooks.com

First edition published 2005

Book design by Elizabeth Rendfleisch

Library of Congress Cataloging-in-Publication Data

Ojakangas, Beatrice A.
Cooking with convection / Beatrice Ojakangas.
p. cm.
1. Convection oven cookery. I. Title.

TX840.C65O35 2004
641.5'8—dc22
2004045123

ISBN 0-7679-1531-3

15   16

Dedicated to my late mother, Esther Luoma,
who taught me how to cook on a woodstove.

Contents

Acknowledgments

"Every river flows into the sea, but the sea is not yet full. The water returns to where the rivers began and starts all over again." These are the words of the philosopher in Ecclesiastes.

After writing some two dozen cookbooks, I was beginning to feel like the water in the rivers. There's no new idea in the world. It's all been done over and over again. But the hope lies in the fact that the sea is not yet full.

I had thought I'd begin to write a memoir—not necessarily to throw into the river of publications, but for my children and grandchildren. Then, whether it was serendipity, or destiny, or just plain good luck, I got a call to present a seminar on convection oven cooking. Here was a river leading to the sea of cookbooks that had not yet been identified or named. I talked with friends, acquaintances, strangers, food editors, and colleagues and found a common issue. Among those who had new or relatively new ovens or ranges in their kitchens, many had the convection option, but few ever used it. They might have tried it once or twice, but with less than exciting results.

There are so many people to thank for their enthusiasm and assistance. For bringing this idea into my consciousness, thanks to the folks at General Electric: Kim Freeman, Mary Taylor, Maria Ladd, Gary Howard, Terry Dunn, Michael McDermott, and Jerry Wolff, to name just a few. Jill Notini at the Association of Home Appliance Manufacturers gathered numbers and statistics for me. For their enthusiasm, Marilyn Sterchi of the Maytag, Jenn-Air Corporation and fellow members of IACP too numerous to mention.

Thanks to my agent, Jane Dystel; my editor, Jennifer Josephy; Allyson Giard; and the staff at Broadway Books, who deserve a huge thank you for their patience with me. Just as I was "coming into the homestretch" writing and testing this book, I was diagnosed with breast cancer. What followed were surgeries, chemo-therapy, and radiation, which slowed me down. Thankfully, Jane and Jennifer agreed that the deadline should be pushed back. And it was.

When a woman I had never seen before, and whose name I still don't know, stepped over from the next line at the supermarket to say "I've been praying for you," I realized I have a whole host of "angels" to thank. By the power of prayer and the best medical help in the world, I am fine.

Introduction

A couple of years ago I was asked to present a seminar on convection oven cooking. Curious, I asked how I happened to be selected for this project. The answer was because I had written a cookbook on countertop convection oven cooking in 1980. It surprised me that there was nothing newer on the market.

I did my own search and found that no book has been published specifically for standard-sized convection ovens. All I could find were books written for countertop convection ovens, one of them my own. Of course, I said yes to the seminar. I was eager to explore the advantages of baking and roasting in the convection oven.

Years ago, a colleague of mine told me, "You don't think you're cooking unless there is an oven involved." I come from a long line of home bakers. My Finnish grandmothers baked in the ovens of wood-fired hearths of rural Finland, in the same style as their mothers and grandmothers. In fact, the first baking I ever did was in the oven of a woodstove. When our first electric range was installed (I was about ten years old), I couldn't keep my hands off it—I thought it was magical.

There was not another significant breakthrough in cooking technology until the convection oven began to be used in commercial kitchens in the 1960s. In the years following my convection oven cookbook, I graduated from countertop models to standard-sized convection ovens and now have three different 30-inch units in my kitchen.

In a convection oven, foods generally cook and brown evenly in considerably less time than in a conventional oven, and at a lower temperature, while retaining juiciness and flavor. Like the "surround sound" of modern music systems, convection ovens produce "surround heat." A fan intensifies the heat by circulating it around the food.

Over the years, I've often spent eight to ten hours a day in the kitchen developing and testing recipes for breads, cakes, pies, cookies, pastries, and fancy desserts, and although I've baked all day and the kitchen counter is piled with goodies, at dinnertime there still may be "nothing to eat"!

What do I do? Rather than resort to take-out or convenience meals, I usually turn up the heat in the convection oven and "hot roast" a quick meal in twenty minutes or less. A variety of roasted fresh vegetables can make a healthy, flavorful meatless meal, or I can choose to add poultry, meat, or fish for a low-fat meal. The variety and selection of ingredients for these meals depends largely on the season, how recently I've been grocery shopping, and what happens to be in the refrigerator at the time. In the winter it might be quickly roasted root vegetables, whereas in the summer it might be roasted ratatouille or other vegetables from the garden.

Much as I love outdoor grilling, in our northern climate it simply isn't possible to grill outdoors all year. I've turned to oven-grilling chicken, chops, steaks, and vegetables, adapting my favorites and using the marinades and bastes we've come to love for the outdoor grill. To make the grill marks I preheat a cast-iron grill pan right along with the oven and oven-grill everything from hamburgers to chicken breasts to fresh vegetables in minutes. Grill pans are widely available in the cookware sections in many superstores, supermarkets, and department stores across the country. Some are flat with a pancake griddle on one side and a ridged grill on the other. Some look like a cast-iron frying pan with ridges across the bottom. Either style works well.

Quickly roasted meals, however, do not tell the whole story about convection oven cooking. I also bake crusty, rustic bread or French baguettes; moist and tender cakes; and all our favorite pies and cookies. Beef, pork, and lamb roasts; turkey and whole chickens; even a whole salmon will cook in a third to half the time of a regular oven. Quiches, gratins, casseroles, and even soufflés turn out perfectly.

Although convection oven cooking seems like something new, professional chefs have been using it for decades in commercial kitchens for its speed and even cooking and browning features. Today these ovens are widely available to home cooks at affordable prices.

I do a lot of cooking in our church's institution-sized kitchen. Several years ago, we sold a thousand tickets for our newly established annual lutefisk, salmon, and meatball dinner. We planned to cook everything in the church's ovens, but we did not have a commercial convection oven, just four conventional commercial ovens that cooked unevenly and on only one rack at a time. We needed a convection oven in which we could cook faster and on six to eight racks at once. Luckily, we located a used commercial convection oven. Two days before our event it arrived, and it was so large that it would not fit through the kitchen doors! The oven had to be disassembled and reassembled in the kitchen, but our "new" convection oven performed like magic. We served all our guests without delays and the dinner was a success, and has been a bigger success every year since. We can thank our convection oven.

There are millions of convection ovens installed in private homes today, but people have had to figure out on their own how to adapt their favorite recipes, with varying degrees of success. This book is here to help!

It wasn't until the late 1700s that the home oven was invented. Before that, baking was done on the open hearth. Gas-fired ovens were introduced in the mid-1800s, and the mid-twentieth century saw the introduction of electric stoves and ovens. No matter what the energy source—wood, gas, or electricity—ovens are essentially hot boxes in which food cooks surrounded by heat.

In a convection oven, a fan circulates air to distribute the heat evenly over, under, and around the food. One can cook on multiple racks at one time in this oven. Because circulating air effectively removes the blanket of cool air that surrounds food in the oven, heat contacts the food immediately. Circulating hot air quickly seals in juices, so smells and flavors don't transfer to other dishes in the oven. In addition, food cooks and browns evenly in less time and almost always at a lower temperature than in a conventional oven.

There are several brands of convection ovens on the market; each has slightly different features. The principles of convection cooking remain the same as long as the oven temperature is true. I've found little difference in oven performance among the various brands. It is helpful, however, to understand the difference among convection oven settings on your range. Here are some of the settings you will find in different brands of ovens and their advantages.

CONVECTION BAKE Check the manual that comes with the oven. The speed of the fan varies and the elements providing the heat will vary from one brand to another. In some ovens set at the convection bake option, the heat comes from a unit that circles the fan in the back of the oven.

CONVECTION ROAST Check the manual that comes with the oven. In some ovens convection roast simply indicates a faster fan speed. In others the source of the heat may vary, but may include heat from the top and bottom of the oven.

CONVECTION BROIL Check the manual that comes with the oven. Some ovens do not include this feature, but recipes that call for convection broiling are interchangeable with convection roast settings.

Adjusting time and temperatures

The recipes in this book that are cooked on the "convection bake" mode are tested for convection temperature, generally 25 degrees lower than conventional baking. The time is slightly reduced, depending on what you are baking. However, the advantage is that you can bake on multiple racks at the same time. This reduces the total baking time of a batch of cookies because you can bake three pans at once. You can also cook three different parts of a meal at one time—chicken or meat, vegetables, and a dessert on a third rack—with excellent results.

The recipes in this book that use the "convection roast" mode might not be cooked at a reduced temperature. However, the cooking time is usually 25 to 30 percent less than conventional roasting time. In some recipes food is cooked at a higher temperature than usual using a "hot roast" technique. Use these recipes as a guide. Generally, the denseness of the food is what determines whether "hot roast" will work well. That is, thick, dense roasts and poultry cook better at a lower temperature. "Hot roast-

ing" is excellent for steaks, chops, fish, ribs, and foods no thicker than 2 to 2^1/2 inches.

Some convection ovens automatically set the temperature 25 degrees lower. For instance, if your favorite recipe indicates a bake temperature of 375°F and you program the oven to "convection bake," it will heat only to 350°F. **Be sure to read your oven's manual for specific information on your oven.**

The recipes in this book need no time or temperature adjustment for convection cooking. All the baking recipes indicate "convection bake" temperature or "convection roast." When using recipes or prepared mixes that give baking time for conventional baking, you will usually need to set the oven 25 degrees lower than the recipe or package directions. Baking time will be the same or a few minutes less.

General guidelines

BAKING PANS Air circulation is the most important factor. As in conventional baking, dark pans or glass baking pans absorb more heat and result in darker browning. Shiny pans will give a lighter product because heat is reflected away from the food. Allow 1 to 1^1/2 inches around pans, including above and below pans, when cooking on more than one rack at a time. Never cover the oven racks with foil. This will block air flow in the oven and reflect heat, which will affect baking time and temperature.

When baking cookies, use rimless (noninsulated) cookie sheets to allow air to circulate around food evenly. Use baking pans with low sides (such as jelly roll pans or half sheet pans) for roasting vegetables or foods that might produce juices that would drip into the oven. Many of the recipes in this book give directions for lining a shallow baking pan with foil. This is simply for cleanup convenience.

Some ovens come with special pans and racks that lift roasts so the air circulates all around. Place the long sides of the pan parallel to the oven door if possible. For easier cleanup, the pan beneath the slotted rack can be lined with foil without affecting roasting time.

Food prepared in covered cookware such as casseroles or foods wrapped in foil do not benefit as much from convection cooking because the air does not touch the food. Large cuts of meat benefit from long, slow convection cooking because convected air seals in the juices while browning the exterior of the roast. This allows a less tender cut of meat, such as a top round of beef, to simmer to tenderness in its own juices.

The recipes in this book are all well tested. Use them as they are, or use them as guides to convert your favorite recipes to convection oven cooking. Where appropriate, chapters begin with a chart showing convection baking and roasting times.

Appetizers and Snacks

Almost any appetizer you would cook on a barbecue grill is a candidate for convection roasting. The flexibility of being able to use the grill regardless of the weather and the speed with which you can prepare delectable appetizers are amazing.

My idea of a perfect quick appetizer or snack is one I can assemble while the oven preheats. Many of the recipes in this chapter will be exactly that—ready for the oven in ten minutes or less.

Roasted Garlic and Parmesan Bread

One 12-inch loaf French bread

¹/₄ cup olive oil

4 garlic cloves, minced

¹/₂ cup freshly grated Parmesan

1. Position the oven racks so that the top rack is in the center of the oven or, if you are tripling the recipe, position the oven racks so they are evenly spaced, with the second rack in the center of the oven. Preheat the oven to convection roast at 500°F.

2. Split the bread in half lengthwise as the oven preheats. Combine the olive oil and garlic and brush the mixture on the cut sides of the bread. Sprinkle with the Parmesan.

3. Place the bread directly on the center rack, cut sides up, and roast for 5 minutes, until lightly toasted.

4. Transfer the bread to a cutting board and cut into 2-inch slices. Serve warm.

This old favorite is a quick snack or accompaniment to a simple soup and salad meal. You can get the bread ready for roasting as the oven preheats. In the summer, I like to serve slices of toasted bread with a topping of chopped or thinly sliced fresh tomatoes from the garden.

■ Makes 4 to 6 servings

Danish Blue Cheese Toasts

$1/2$ cup crumbled blue cheese

$1/2$ cup grated mozzarella

2 tablespoons toasted pine nuts, chopped walnuts,
or slivered almonds

1 garlic clove, minced

Freshly ground black pepper

Twenty-four $1/2$-inch slices coarse-textured Italian
or French bread

$1/4$ cup olive oil or melted butter

Serve these toasts hot out of the oven. They're a real crowd-pleaser and the recipe is easy to multiply to serve lots of people. If you make three panfuls at a time, position the oven racks so that they are evenly spaced and bake all three at once.

■ Makes about 8 servings
(3 pieces each)

1. Position the oven racks so that the top rack is in the center of the oven or, if you are tripling the recipe, position the oven racks so they are evenly spaced, with the second rack in the center of the oven. Preheat the oven to convection roast at 500°F.

2. While the oven is preheating, combine the blue cheese, mozzarella, pine nuts, garlic, and pepper in a bowl. Brush each slice of bread with olive oil and place on a rimless cookie sheet. Roast the bread on the center rack for 3 to 5 minutes, until toasted on one side. Remove the bread from the oven and turn over. Spread each slice with the cheese mixture, pressing down slightly with a fork.

3. Return the bread to the oven and roast until the cheese mixture has melted. Serve immediately.

Oven-Roasted Cheese Quesadillas

This is a great quick snack or appetizer. To make it a bit heartier, add more toppings like chopped green onions, diced peppers, bits of sausage, or additional cheese. ■ Makes 4 to 6 servings

Four 10-inch flour tortillas

2 tablespoons corn oil

2 cups shredded Monterey Jack or mild Cheddar

Salsa, homemade or store-bought

Chopped fresh cilantro for garnish

1. Position the oven racks so that the top rack is in the center of the oven or, if you are tripling the recipe, position the oven racks so they are evenly spaced, with the second rack in the center of the oven. Preheat the oven to convection bake at 500°F. Have a rimless cookie sheet ready.

2. While the oven is preheating, assemble the quesadillas. Lightly brush 2 tortillas with some of the oil on one side. Place the tortillas next to each other, oiled side down on the cookie sheet.

3. Top each with 1 cup of the cheese and cover each with another tortilla. Press down lightly to compress the cheese. Lightly brush the top of each quesadilla with the remaining oil.

4. Place the cookie sheet on the center rack of the oven. Watch the quesadillas closely, and as soon as the cheese begins to melt, press down lightly on each quesadilla with a spatula and turn them over to brown the other side. Remove the quesadillas from the oven when browned on both sides.

5. Transfer the quesadillas to a cutting board and, using a large, sharp knife, cut each one into 4 to 6 wedges. Top the wedges with salsa and a sprinkling of cilantro. Serve warm.

Baked Potato Skins Stuffed with Bacon and Cheese

3 medium russet potatoes

Vegetable oil

5 bacon slices

Kosher salt and freshly ground black pepper

1^1/4 cups shredded sharp Cheddar

1^1/4 cups shredded Monterey Jack

1 tablespoon chopped fresh flat-leaf parsley

^{1}/4 teaspoon cayenne pepper

^{1}/4 cup chopped fresh chives

Sour cream

1. Position the oven racks so that they are evenly spaced. Preheat the oven to convection roast at 425°F. Scrub the potatoes and pat dry; poke each one with a fork to break the skin. Coat them lightly with oil and place them directly on the top rack.

2. Spread the bacon slices on a baking pan with a shallow rim and place the pan on the center rack. Bake the potatoes for 30 to 35 minutes, until a skewer inserted into the centers comes out clean and dry. Remove the potatoes and bacon from the oven.

3. Cut the potatoes in half and scoop out the centers, leaving a ^{1}/2-inch layer of cooked potato in the skins. (Reserve the scooped-out flesh for another use, such as mashed potatoes.) Place the skins, skin side down, about 1 inch apart on a shallow baking pan and sprinkle them with salt and black pepper.

4. Drain and crumble the bacon and transfer to a medium mixing bowl. Add the cheeses, parsley, and cayenne and stir to blend. Fill the potato skins with the mixture. Bake on the center rack until the skins are crisp and the cheese mixture melts, about 10 minutes.

5. Transfer the skins to a serving platter and top with the chives and dollops of sour cream.

The convection oven makes easy work of this recipe. While you roast the potatoes, cook the bacon in the convection oven. This leaves your cooktop splatter free.

■ Makes 6 appetizer or first-course servings

Oven-drying concentrates the flavor and aroma of tomatoes, something I like to do especially in the winter, when fresh tomatoes are not always flavorful. In the convection oven, the tomatoes dry in about half the time of a conventional oven. You can store the dried tomatoes in the refrigerator for up to 3 days. Otherwise, wrap them well and freeze them for later use. I love them served this way: simply topped with fresh mozzarella and seasonings on a crisp crouton. They're great in salads, or as an accompaniment for oven-grilled chicken breasts. ■ Makes 24 appetizers

Oven-Dried Tomatoes with Fresh Mozzarella

12 small plum (Roma) tomatoes
$^1/_2$ teaspoon kosher salt
$^1/_2$ pound fresh mozzarella, sliced
Balsamic vinegar
24 fresh basil leaves or dried basil
24 croutons or French bread slices, about
    $2^1/_2$ inches in diameter

1. Position the oven racks so that the top rack is in the center of the oven or, if you are tripling the recipe, position the oven racks so they are evenly spaced, with the second rack in the center of the oven. Preheat the oven to convection bake at 250°F. Cover a baking sheet with parchment paper.

2. Cut each tomato in half lengthwise and place the halves on the prepared baking sheet, cut sides up. Sprinkle them with the salt.

3. Place the tomatoes in the oven and dry for $2^1/_2$ to 3 hours or until the tomatoes are shriveled around the edges but still juicy.

4. Top each tomato with a small slice of mozzarella, drizzle with balsamic vinegar, and top with a basil leaf, if available, or a light sprinkling of dried basil. Serve on top of a crouton or a slice of crusty French bread.

Spiced Chicken Bites

6 skinless, boneless chicken breast halves

12 tablespoons (1^1/2 sticks) butter, melted

2 garlic cloves, minced

1 cup fine dried bread crumbs

^{1}/2 cup freshly grated Parmesan

1 teaspoon fresh thyme

^{1}/2 teaspoon kosher salt

1 teaspoon ancho or chipotle chile powder
    (page 47) or red pepper flakes

1. Position the oven racks so that the top rack is in the center of the oven. Preheat the oven to convection roast at 450°F. Cover a shallow baking pan with foil and coat with nonstick spray.

2. Cut the chicken into 2-inch cubes. Combine the butter and garlic in a shallow dish. Combine the bread crumbs, Parmesan, thyme, salt, and chile powder in another dish. Roll the chicken first in the butter mixture and then in the bread crumb mixture. Place the chicken pieces half an inch apart on the prepared baking pan. Put the pan on the center rack.

3. Roast the chicken for 10 to 12 minutes, until it is cooked and the crumbs are lightly browned.

These little cubes of chicken resemble chicken nuggets and are perfect when you're trying to think of something to feed children. Eliminate the hot spices if the kids object (but one of my granddaughters announced, "I like hot!").

■ Makes 12 to 16 appetizer or
6 main-dish servings

Spicy Chicken Drummettes

FOR THE MARINADE

$^1/_2$ **cup soy sauce**

$^1/_3$ **cup honey**

1 tablespoon cornstarch

2 teaspoons freshly squeezed lemon juice

1 teaspoon curry powder

$^1/_2$ **teaspoon red pepper flakes, optional**

1 teaspoon ground ginger

2 pounds chicken drummettes (about 26 pieces)

$^1/_3$ **cup sesame seeds**

Chicken-wing drumsticks are a favorite appetizer and are so quick and easy to prepare and cook in the convection oven. For a bit more fire, add crushed red pepper flakes to the marinade.

■ Makes 12–13 appetizer servings

1. To make the marinade, in a small saucepan, combine the soy sauce, honey, cornstarch, lemon juice, curry powder, red pepper flakes, if using, and ginger; stir to dissolve the cornstarch. Cook the mixture over medium heat until it boils and thickens, about 2 minutes. Cool the mixture.

2. Place the chicken in a heavy zip-top plastic bag; pour the cooled marinade over it. Refrigerate for at least 1 hour or as long as overnight.

3. Arrange the oven racks so that they are evenly spaced. Preheat the oven to convection roast at 425°F. Line the bottom of a two-piece broiler pan or a shallow sheet pan with foil. Coat the foil with nonstick spray. Place the chicken in the pan. Sprinkle it with sesame seeds and bake in the center of the oven for 20 to 25 minutes, until browned.

Roast-Dried Cauliflower and Broccoli Florets with Dipping Sauces

1 small head cauliflower

1 small head broccoli

Kosher salt and freshly ground black pepper

Hot Garlic-Anchovy Dipping Sauce (recipe follows)

Teriyaki Dipping Sauce (recipe follows)

Creamy Garlic Ranch Sauce (recipe follows)

1. Position the oven racks so that they are evenly spaced. Preheat the oven to convection bake at 225°F. Cover two or three rimless baking sheets with parchment paper.

2. Trim the leaves off the cauliflower and cut the head into quarters. Cut the cauliflower into florets, leaving no more than 2 inches of core.

3. Trim the tough ends from the broccoli and cut it into florets, leaving no more than 2 inches of stem on each.

4. Arrange the vegetables on the baking sheets and sprinkle with salt and pepper. Place the pans on the oven racks and convection bake for 30 minutes.

5. Transfer the vegetables to serving bowls and serve with a variety of dipping sauces.

Hot Garlic-Anchovy Dipping Sauce

Keep this sauce over a candle-warmer for the best flavor, but you can assemble the ingredients hours ahead. You can find anchovy paste in the gourmet section of most supermarkets. Otherwise, substitute half a tin of anchovy fillets, mashed. ■ Makes about $1/3$ cup

4 tablespoons ($1/2$ stick) butter

2 tablespoons olive oil

2 garlic cloves, minced

1 tablespoon anchovy paste

Combine all the ingredients in a small saucepan and place over a candle-warmer or very low heat. The mixture must not get so hot that it burns.

Teriyaki Dipping Sauce

If you make this ahead of time, keep it refrigerated but bring it to room temperature before serving. ■ Makes about $2/3$ cup

$1/2$ cup rice wine vinegar or dry sherry

2 tablespoons soy sauce

4 teaspoons sugar

1 teaspoon peeled and grated fresh ginger, or
 $1/4$ teaspoon ground

1 green onion, thinly sliced crosswise including
 green part

In a small saucepan, combine all the ingredients, except the green onion, with $3/4$ cup water. Bring to a boil, remove from the heat, and cool. Add the green onion.

Creamy Garlic Ranch Sauce

This is a quickly assembled dipping sauce from ingredients you might have on hand.

■ Makes about 1 cup

1 cup Ranch-style creamy salad dressing

1 garlic clove, minced

$1/4$ cup chopped fresh flat-leaf parsley

Combine all the ingredients in a bowl and serve.

Cauliflower and broccoli florets turn out crisp around the edges and chewy in the center when dried in the convection oven at a low temperature. Serve them warm from the oven with one or a selection of the suggested dipping sauces. The cauliflower and broccoli are best served freshly roasted, but the dipping sauces can be made several hours ahead and refrigerated.

■ Makes 12 to 16 servings

Simple to make, the unfilled cream puffs freeze easily, then can be reheated and stuffed with this tasty smoked salmon filling just before serving. You can also serve the cream puffs for dessert filled with vanilla ice cream and covered with chocolate sauce—the French bistro classic, profiteroles. ■ Makes 30 appetizers

Baby Cream Puffs Filled with Smoked Salmon

FOR THE CREAM PUFFS

4 tablespoons ($^1/_2$ stick) butter

$^1/_2$ cup all-purpose flour

2 eggs

FOR THE FILLING

4 tablespoons ($^1/_2$ stick) butter, softened

2 teaspoons minced fresh chives

$^1/_2$ teaspoon minced fresh tarragon, or
   $^1/_4$ teaspoon dried

$^1/_2$ cup finely minced smoked salmon

1. Position the oven racks so that they are evenly spaced. Preheat the oven to convection bake at 400°F. Cover a rimless cookie sheet with parchment paper or lightly grease a cookie sheet.

2. To make the cream puffs, melt the butter in $^1/_2$ cup boiling water in a saucepan over high heat. Add the flour all at once and stir until the mixture forms a solid mass. Cool for 3 to 4 minutes. Beat in the eggs one at a time and stir until the batter is smooth and glossy.

3. Scoop heaping teaspoonfuls of the dough onto the cookie sheet, spacing them about $1^1/_2$ inches apart.

4. Bake on the center rack for 10 minutes, then reduce the oven temperature to 325°F. Bake for 5 more minutes or until the cream puffs are dry and golden. Let cool.

5. To make the filling, stir together the butter, chives, tarragon, and smoked salmon while the cream puffs bake.

6. Fill the cooled cream puffs with the mixture just before serving.

Roasted garlic becomes sweet, losing the sharp pungency that makes raw garlic so powerful. You can spread roasted garlic like butter on bread or vegetables. Add it to soups, sauces, and dressings, or smear it onto a pizza. You can roast a number of whole heads at one time.

Whole Roasted Garlic Heads

Whole garlic heads
Olive oil

1. Position the oven racks so that they are evenly spaced. Preheat the oven to convection roast at 400°F.

2. Place the garlic heads side by side on a sheet of foil and drizzle them with olive oil. Wrap them tightly in foil and place on a baking sheet. Roast the heads on the center rack for 35 to 40 minutes or until the garlic is very soft.

3. Let the garlic cool, still wrapped. To serve, un-wrap and squeeze individual garlic cloves from their skins into a bowl or onto bread, crackers, or vegetables.

Pizza and Pasta

Pizza and focaccia depend on a hot blast of air for the best crust texture. As with everything else cooked in the convection oven, baking time is shortened. A pre-heated pizza stone increases the crispiness of the bottom crust. Place the stone (or squares of unglazed tiles) on a rack positioned in the center of the oven as you pre-heat it. You can either slip the ready-to-bake pizza or focaccia directly onto the stone or, if you have trouble handling pizza that way, place it on a dark, noninsulated cookie sheet for excellent results.

The recipes in this chapter offer a handful of topping suggestions. I have a stack of cookbooks a foot high devoted just to pizzas, and they don't begin to cover all the possible varieties.

A few guidelines:

- Have all the toppings ready before rolling out the dough.
- Don't get carried away with too many toppings, usually three or four work better than a large number of flavors. When you're being creative, it helps to think of pizza as a hot open-faced sandwich.
- Use cheese that melts easily and shred it so that you can distribute it evenly over the pizza. Mozzarella and Monterey Jack work well.
- You don't always have to cover pizza dough with a tomato sauce. For a change try using a coating of olive oil or a thin layer of prepared pesto sauce.
- You can design your own homemade crust by varying the flour, herbs, and

other seasonings used. Also, consider making extra crusts. Roll them out on foil and freeze them. Once frozen solid, wrap them well in another sheet of foil to prevent drying out. Frozen pizza crusts keep for several weeks.

Pasta casseroles speak of "down home," everyday favorite foods. They're still the subject of many potluck gatherings, but here I suggest casseroles and one-dish meals with an up-to-date flair. The convenience of these dishes is that many of them can be assembled, or assembled, baked, and chilled, ready for reheating later.

Many casseroles can be frozen in individual serving containers or in containers with tight-fitting lids, in zip-top plastic bags, or wrapped in heavy-duty foil. Of course, they should be labeled and dated. Thaw frozen foods in the refrigerator, and be sure to remove wrappings before baking them.

There are temperature and time adjustments to make when convection baking these foods for the best results, so heed the instructions carefully.

For pizza lovers, here are eight varieties to choose from. The basic dough makes two pizzas. The dough is easy to mix in the food processor.

■ Makes two 12-inch pizzas

One Basic Dough and Eight Pizzas

FOR THE PIZZA DOUGH

2^1/3 cups unbleached all-purpose flour

1 teaspoon salt

2^1/4 teaspoons (1 package) active dry yeast

1 tablespoon olive oil

1. To make the pizza dough, measure the flour, salt, and yeast into the bowl of a food processor fitted with the steel blade. Turn the processor on and slowly add the water and olive oil; process until the dough is smooth (the dough will be soft). Or to mix by hand, measure the flour and combine it with the salt and yeast in a mixing bowl. Stir 1 cup warm (105° to 115°F) water and the olive oil into the flour mixture; blend thoroughly. Turn out onto a floured board.

2. Lightly knead the soft dough until smooth. Place the dough in a greased bowl; cover with plastic wrap and let it rise for 50 to 60 minutes or until doubled.

3. Place a pizza stone on the center rack of the oven. Preheat the oven to convection bake at 450°F. *(continued)*

4. Punch the dough down; divide it in half. On a floured surface, roll each piece into a 12-inch circle. Cut two 15- to 16-inch squares of heavy-duty foil. Coat them with nonstick spray. Place the dough in the center of each square of foil, and with floured hands pat them into 12-inch rounds. Let the dough rise for 20 minutes. Top each with one of the suggested toppings that follow.

5. Transfer the pizzas onto the heated pizza stone in the oven. Bake them for 12 to 15 minutes, until the edges are browned and the toppings are bubbly.

Tomato, Basil, and Mozzarella Pizza

Slice one small red onion thinly and spread it over the pizza dough. Cover the onion with 2 thinly sliced tomatoes. Season the topping with kosher salt and freshly ground black pepper. Sprinkle 2 to 3 finely chopped garlic cloves on top. Cut 4 ounces of fresh mozzarella into small pieces and sprinkle over the pizza. After baking, drizzle the pizza with 1 tablespoon olive oil and sprinkle it with $1/4$ cup finely shredded fresh basil leaves.

Barbecued Chicken Pizza

Spread the pizza dough with $1/2$ cup prepared barbecue sauce, and distribute one thinly sliced small red onion, $3/4$ cup shredded cooked chicken, and 1 cup (4 ounces) shredded mozzarella evenly over the sauce.

Pesto Pizza

Spread $1/2$ cup prepared basil pesto over the pizza dough to within $1/2$ inch of the edge. Arrange one $2^1/2$-ounce can drained, sliced black olives over the pesto layer. Drain one 6-ounce jar marinated artichoke hearts and chop them. Spread them evenly over the olives. Top with $1^1/2$ cups crumbled goat cheese.

Sun-Dried Tomato, Basil, and Mushroom Pizza

Drain $1/3$ cup oil-packed sun-dried tomatoes and cut them into small strips. Arrange them evenly over the pizza dough. Drizzle with 1 to 2 teaspoons of the tomato oil over all. Sprinkle with 2 minced garlic cloves, $1/4$ cup shredded fresh basil leaves, 2 tablespoons pine nuts, and $1/2$ cup sliced fresh mushrooms. Sprinkle with 2 tablespoons freshly grated Parmesan and top with half a medium red bell pepper, seeded and sliced into thin strips.

Greek Pizza

Spread the pizza dough with $1/2$ cup prepared pesto sauce. Top with 4 thinly sliced plum (Roma) tomatoes, 1 tablespoon chopped garlic, and 4 cups loosely packed fresh baby spinach. Sprinkle with 4 ounces crumbled feta.

Primavera Pizza

Spread the pizza dough with 2 tablespoons light olive oil. Top with 1 small, thinly sliced red onion; 1 small orange bell pepper, seeded and cut into thin strips; 1 small zucchini, thinly sliced into ribbons; 12 fresh asparagus spears, cut into 2-inch pieces; 4 finely chopped garlic cloves; and 8 ounces fresh mozzarella, cut into thin sticks.

Roasted Onion, Rosemary, and Blue Cheese Pizza

Spread the pizza dough with 4 large roasted onions (see Caramelized Roasted Onions, page 130), 2 teaspoons fresh rosemary leaves, $2/3$ cup chopped walnuts, and $3/4$ cup crumbled blue cheese.

Roasted Vegetable Pizza

Preheat the oven to 450°F. In a large bowl, toss together 2 sliced plum (Roma) tomatoes, 1 sliced and seeded red bell pepper, 1 medium zucchini, cut into $1/2$-inch cubes, and 1 small red onion, thinly sliced, with 2 tablespoons olive oil. Spread on a large, rimmed baking sheet and convection roast on the center rack for 10 minutes or until softened and browned. Remove from the oven. Let cool. Top the pizza dough with the vegetables and sprinkle with 1 cup shredded mozzarella.

This delicious flat bread is great cut into 1- to 2-inch squares and served as an appetizer or cut into larger squares to accompany soups and salads. You can create tasty variations by trying different cheese combinations, such as Cheddar, Swiss, or Monterey Jack, or by changing the herbs to oregano and parsley, or chives and shallots.

■ Makes about 5 dozen appetizers or 8 large squares

Four-Cheese Stuffed Focaccia

FOR THE DOUGH

$2^1/4$ teaspoons (1 package) active dry yeast

4 cups unsifted bread flour

1 teaspoon sugar

1 teaspoon salt

1 tablespoon olive oil

FOR THE FILLING

2 to 3 garlic cloves, minced

$1/2$ teaspoon fresh rosemary, slightly crushed

2 tablespoons finely chopped fresh basil

1 cup (4 ounces) shredded Provolone

1 cup (4 ounces) shredded Gouda

1 cup (4 ounces) shredded Jarlsberg

$1/4$ cup freshly grated Parmesan

$1/4$ cup roasted red pepper, cut into $1/4$-inch dice

FOR THE TOPPING

2 tablespoons olive oil

2 tablespoons finely chopped fresh basil

$1/4$ cup freshly grated Parmesan

1. To make the dough, pour $^1/4$ cup warm (110° to 115°F) water into a small, shallow bowl; sprinkle in the yeast. Stir to dissolve the yeast completely.

2. Combine the flour, sugar, and salt in a large mixing bowl. Add the yeast mixture, $1^1/4$ cups warm water, and the olive oil to the flour mixture and blend thoroughly.

3. Turn the dough out onto a floured board. Knead it until smooth and elastic, about 10 minutes. Place the dough in a greased bowl; cover the bowl with plastic wrap and let rise for 50 to 60 minutes or until the dough has doubled.

4. Position the oven racks so that they are evenly spaced, with one rack in the center of the oven. Preheat the oven to convection bake at 350°F.

5. Punch the dough down and divide it in half. Roll the first half of the dough to fit the bottom and sides of an ungreased $12^1/2 \times 17^1/2$-inch baking pan. Sprinkle with the garlic, rosemary, 2 tablespoons basil, Provolone, Gouda, Jarlsberg, and $^1/4$ cup Parmesan. Evenly distribute the pepper strips over the cheeses.

6. Roll out the second half of the dough. Place it on top of the cheeses and pepper. Press the edges of the bottom and top crusts together to seal. Brush the top with olive oil and sprinkle it evenly with the remaining 2 tablespoons basil and $^1/4$ cup Parmesan. Using your fingertips or knuckle, firmly press dimples into the dough at 1-inch intervals. Cover the focaccia with a towel and allow it to rise in the oven, as above, for 20 to 30 minutes or until puffy.

7. Bake the focaccia for 20 to 25 minutes on the center rack, until lightly browned.

Rosemary Focaccia with Onions, Black Olives, and Sun-Dried Tomatoes

FOR THE DOUGH

$2^1/2$ to 3 cups unsifted bread flour

$1/4$ cup fresh rosemary leaves, or 2 tablespoons
dried

4 garlic cloves, minced

1 tablespoon sugar

$1^1/2$ teaspoons salt

$2^1/4$ teaspoons (1 package) active dry yeast

2 tablespoons extra virgin olive oil

FOR THE TOPPING

1 white onion, sliced into thin rings

2 tablespoons extra virgin olive oil

$1/4$ cup freshly grated Parmesan

$1/2$ cup whole black olives, drained

$1/2$ cup oil-packed sun-dried tomatoes, well
drained and julienned

1. To make the dough, combine the flour, rosemary, garlic, sugar, salt, and yeast in the bowl of a food processor fitted with the steel blade. Turn the processor on and slowly add 1 cup warm (about 130°F) water through the feed tube; process until blended, then add the olive oil. Process until the dough comes together and spins around the bowl, cleaning the sides. Add 1 to 2 more tablespoons water if the dough feels dry, which can happen when flour is held under very dry conditions. The dough should be soft and moist.

2. Place the dough in an oiled bowl, turning to coat all sides. Cover with plastic wrap and let it rise in a warm place until doubled, about 1 hour.

3. Position the oven racks so that they are evenly spaced, with one rack in the center of the oven. Preheat the oven to convection bake at 350°F. Coat a shallow roasting pan with nonstick

spray. To make the topping, toss the onion with 1 tablespoon of the olive oil and spread it out in the pan. Bake on the top or center rack for 15 minutes, until the onion is soft. Remove from the oven and let cool.

4. Spread the remaining 1 tablespoon oil over a 15 × 10 × 1-inch baking pan and turn the risen dough out onto it. With oiled hands, press the dough to the edges of the pan. Cover and let it rise for 30 minutes.

5. Increase the oven temperature to 475°F. Sprinkle the dough with the Parmesan.

6. Press the olives down into the dough (they will break into pieces). Arrange the cooled onion over the dough and press it in firmly, then press the sun-dried tomatoes into the dough.

7. Bake for 13 to 15 minutes, until the edges are golden. Serve hot, cut into 3-inch squares.

This focaccia adds onions, olives, and dried tomatoes to the top. Cut into bite-sized pieces, it's a great appetizer. The dough mixes most easily in a food processor.

■ Makes one 15 × 10-inch focaccia

Kids love "mac and cheese." When I make it from scratch, I know what's in it—all healthy ingredients! Here's how to do it, saving time and energy in the convection oven. ■ Makes 6 servings

Macaroni and Cheese

4 tablespoons ($^1/_2$ stick) butter, plus 1 tablespoon for the casserole

3 slices homemade-style white bread, crusts removed and torn into $^1/_2$-inch pieces

$^1/_4$ cup all-purpose flour

$2^3/_4$ cups hot whole or 2% milk

1 teaspoon kosher salt

$^1/_8$ teaspoon freshly grated nutmeg

$^1/_8$ teaspoon freshly ground black pepper

Pinch cayenne pepper

2 cups shredded Cheddar

$1^1/_2$ cups shredded Fontina or Swiss cheese

$^1/_2$ pound elbow macaroni

1. Position the oven racks so that they are evenly spaced, with one rack in the center of the oven. Preheat the oven to convection bake at 350°F. Butter a $1^1/_2$-quart casserole and set aside.

2. Melt the 4 tablespoons butter in a medium saucepan. Spoon 1 tablespoon of the melted butter over the bread crumbs in a small bowl and toss until the bread crumbs are thoroughly coated; set aside.

3. Stir the flour into the remaining 3 tablespoons melted butter over medium heat and cook for 1 minute, stirring.

4. Whisk in the hot milk, keeping the mixture smooth. Cook until the mixture bubbles and thickens, whisking all the time, about 5 minutes.

5. Remove from the heat and stir in the salt, nutmeg, and the black and cayenne peppers. Stir in the Cheddar and Fontina. Set aside.

6. Cook the macaroni according to the package directions, adding salt as directed. When done, drain and add to the cheese sauce. Pour the macaroni into the buttered casserole. Sprinkle with the bread crumbs and bake in the center of the oven until the crumbs are golden, about 20 minutes. Serve hot.

Lasagna with Spinach and Three Cheeses

$1/2$ pound ground beef

$1/2$ pound Italian sausage

$1/4$ pound sliced fresh mushrooms

1 medium onion, chopped

2 garlic cloves, minced

Two 6-ounce cans tomato paste

One $14^1/2$-ounce can diced tomatoes and their
   liquid

$1^1/2$ teaspoons dried basil

$1^1/2$ teaspoons dried oregano

$3/4$ teaspoon kosher salt

$1/4$ teaspoon red pepper flakes

One 8- to 9-ounce package lasagna noodles

One 9-ounce package frozen, chopped spinach,
   drained

One 15-ounce container ricotta

2 eggs

4 cups shredded mozzarella

$1/2$ cup freshly grated Parmesan

You can use any dried lasagna noodles in this easy no-boil method, just be sure that the noodles themselves are completely covered with the filling and sauce.

■ Makes 6 to 8 large servings

1. Position the oven racks so that the top rack is in the center of the oven. Preheat the oven to convection bake at 350°F. Coat a 13 × 9 × 3-inch lasagna pan with nonstick spray.

2. Crumble the ground beef and the sausage meat into a large skillet, add the mushrooms, onion, and garlic, and cook over medium-high heat, stirring occasionally, until the meat is no longer pink. Drain off any fat. Add the tomato paste, $1^1/2$ cups water, the tomatoes and their liquid, basil, oregano, salt, and red pepper flakes; mix well.

3. Spoon about 1 cup of the sauce into the bottom of the baking pan. Top with one-third of the noodles. Spoon 1 cup of sauce over the noodles. Mix the spinach, ricotta, eggs, and half of the mozzarella together and spread one-third of the mixture over the sauce layer.

4. Top with half of the remaining noodles. Repeat layering sauce, the spinach mixture, and noodles, ending with the sauce, and spreading it completely over the pasta; sprinkle the top with the remaining mozzarella and Parmesan. Cover the pan with foil and bake on the center rack of the oven for 45 to 55 minutes or until the pasta is tender and the edges are bubbly. Remove the foil and bake for 5 more minutes or until the top is lightly browned. Let it stand for 15 minutes before serving.

Roasting brings out the sweetness of vegetables and intensifies their fresh flavors. Vary the vegetables if you wish, but follow this general pattern: Roast the vegetables, remove skins if necessary, puree, and flavor the puree with fresh herbs or garlic. Serve over hot pasta or use as a sauce for lasagna. ■ Makes 6 servings

Roasted Onion, Red Pepper, and Tomato Sauce for Pasta

4 red bell peppers, cored, seeded, and quartered

4 tablespoons plus 1 teaspoon olive oil

2 onions, sliced

2 medium, firm tomatoes

3 large garlic cloves, unpeeled

1 teaspoon fresh thyme

1 teaspoon kosher salt

$1/2$ teaspoon freshly ground black pepper

1 pound cooked small pasta, such as penne, or
    filled pasta, such as ravioli

Freshly grated Parmesan

1. Position the oven racks so that they are evenly spaced. Preheat the oven to convection roast at 500°F. Cover a shallow-rimmed baking pan with foil and coat with nonstick spray.

2. Rub the pepper quarters with 2 tablespoons of the olive oil and place on the pan on the top rack of the oven, skin side up. Roast for about 5 minutes, until the peppers are blistered. With tongs, remove and stack them in a paper bag. Let them cool in the bag for 15 minutes.

3. Toss the sliced onions and the whole tomatoes with 2 tablespoons of the olive oil and spread on the prepared pan. Lightly rub the garlic cloves with the remaining 1 teaspoon olive oil and place on the pan. Roast for 5 to 6 minutes, until the onions are lightly browned and soft. Do not remove them from the baking pan.

4. Slip the skins off the tomatoes. Rub the skins off the pepper quarters. Add the tomatoes and peppers to the onions and return to the oven. Roast for 5 more minutes, until the juices are thickened.

5. Scoop all the vegetables into a food processor fitted with the steel blade or a blender (you may need to do this in batches), and process them until almost pureed, but still slightly chunky. Add the thyme, salt, and pepper. Serve over freshly cooked pasta and top with the Parmesan.

Roasted Eggplant and Zucchini Sauce for Pasta

1 eggplant, cut into 2-inch pieces

3 small zucchini, cut into 2-inch pieces

3 large garlic cloves, minced

1 large sweet onion, cut into 2-inch chunks

4 medium tomatoes, cored and left whole

3 tablespoons olive oil

1 teaspoon kosher salt

1/2 teaspoon freshly ground black pepper

Fresh or dried pasta, such as fettuccine, or small pasta, such as ziti or penne

1/2 cup freshly grated Parmesan

Eggplant, zucchini, sweet onions, and tomatoes all roasted together thicken by themselves to make a deeply flavored sauce for pasta. It's a meal that's ready in less than half an hour. ■ Makes 6 servings

1. Position the oven racks so that they are evenly spaced. Preheat the oven to convection roast at 450°F. Cover a large, rimmed pan with foil and coat with nonstick spray.

2. In a large bowl, combine the eggplant, zucchini, garlic, onion, and tomatoes and drizzle with the olive oil, salt, and pepper. Spread the vegetables on the prepared pan and roast in the center or top of the oven until the vegetables are soft, about 15 minutes.

3. With tongs, lift the skins off the tomatoes. Return the tomatoes to the pan with the vegetables and roast for 5 more minutes. Scoop the hot vegetables into a food processor or blender fitted with the steel blade. Process just until the vegetables are coarsely chopped and pour them into a serving bowl. You may need to do this in batches.

4. Meanwhile, cook the pasta according to the package directions. Put the pasta into a serving bowl and top it with the vegetable sauce. Serve with the Parmesan.

Savory Pies, Tarts, and Soufflés

Years ago, when quiches were new to home cooks, I taught a very popular quiche class. When eggs became associated with high cholesterol, quiches fell from favor but are now making a comeback. Eggs are again a part of a healthy diet, although quiche will probably always be seen as a delightful indulgence.

I've baked savory pies and tarts in the convection oven and find the results to be superior to baking in a conventional oven. Here is a handful of my favorites, starting with the basic quiche, the beginning of it all.

I bake all pies and tarts in the center of the oven; when I bake three to nine at once, I stagger them on all three racks.

Soufflés seem like magic. They impress and surprise dinner guests—family or friends. They're actually not difficult, and are among the most economical foods. Basically, you cook up a thickened mixture of flour and milk, add flavoring and egg yolks, egg whites are whipped and gently mixed in, then you turn the whole mixture into a dish for baking. Here's where the convection oven does wonders. Soufflés actually bake more quickly and remain high and puffy longer (thanks to how firm the interior becomes) than when you bake them in a conventional oven. That doesn't mean that you can hold the soufflés half an hour for serving—you should have your guests at the table when the soufflé is ready. Here is a sampling of soufflés that range from main dishes to side dishes to desserts.

Classic Quiche Lorraine

Half recipe Flaky Pastry (page 37)

10 slices bacon, cooked crisp, drained well, and
    crumbled

1 1/4 cups (6 ounces) diced or shredded Gruyère or
    Swiss cheese

4 eggs

1 3/4 cups light cream or undiluted evaporated milk
    (not condensed)

Freshly grated nutmeg

1. Position the oven racks so that they are evenly spaced, with one rack in the center of the oven. Preheat the oven to convection bake at 400°F.

2. Line a 9-inch pie or tart pan with the pastry, pinch the edges of the pastry to flute, line the bottom with foil, and weight down with pie weights (uncooked dried beans work well). Bake on the center rack for 15 minutes or until the edges are lightly browned. Remove from the oven; remove the pie weights (you can do this by simply lifting them in the foil out of the pan). Cool on a wire rack.

3. Reduce the oven temperature to 325°F. Evenly distribute the bacon and Gruyère on the bottom of the pastry shell. Beat the eggs and cream together until blended and pour over the Gruyère. Grate the nutmeg over the filling.

4. Bake the quiche on the center rack for 30 to 35 minutes, until the custard is set (a knife inserted just off center will come out clean). Cool on a wire rack. Cut into wedges to serve.

The quiche originated in Alsace-Lorraine, in northeastern France. It's a pastry shell filled with a savory custard of eggs, cream, and other ingredients. Quiche Lorraine always includes crisp bacon with optional cheese. Of course, there are many ways to vary this basic recipe and a few ideas follow. In the convection oven, the temperature is reduced by 25 to 50 degrees and the baking time is reduced as well.

■ Makes 6 to 8 servings

Flaky Pastry

2 cups all-purpose flour

$3/4$ cup ($1^1/2$ sticks) chilled butter, cut into $1/2$-inch pieces

1 egg yolk

2 teaspoons freshly squeezed lemon juice

3 to 4 tablespoons ice water

This is a wonderfully flaky, buttery pastry. For a single-crust pastry, use half the ingredients, but don't halve the egg yolk. You will need slightly less than half the amount of ice water to mix the dough.

■ Makes one 9-inch double-crust pie

1. Put the flour into the bowl of a food processor fitted with the steel blade. Add the butter and process, using on/off pulses, just until the mixture resembles coarse cornmeal. Put the mixture into a large bowl.

2. Combine the egg yolk, lemon juice, and 2 tablespoons of the water. Drizzle this over the flour mixture; toss with a fork or spatula until the dough comes together in a ball, adding the remaining water if necessary. Smooth the ball and press it into a disk shape. Wrap the dough in plastic wrap, and refrigerate for 2 hours or overnight.

Spinach and Ricotta Tart

Half recipe Flaky Pastry (page 37)

2 tablespoons finely minced shallots

2 tablespoons butter

1 pound fresh spinach

$1/2$ teaspoon salt

$1/8$ teaspoon freshly ground black pepper

1 cup ricotta

3 eggs

$1/2$ cup light cream or undiluted evaporated milk
   (not condensed)

$1/4$ cup shredded Swiss cheese

1. Prepare the pastry shell for Classic Quiche Lorraine (page 36).

2. Position the oven racks so that they are evenly spaced. Set the oven temperature to convection bake at 325°F.

3. In a large skillet or deep saucepan, cook the shallots in 1 tablespoon of the butter until soft, about 2 minutes. Add the spinach, cover, and steam for 3 to 5 minutes, until the spinach is wilted but not overcooked. Stir over medium-high heat for a few minutes to evaporate all the liquid.

4. Put the shallot-spinach mixture into a large bowl and add the salt, pepper, ricotta, eggs, and cream. Pour this into the baked pastry shell and sprinkle with the Swiss cheese; dot with the remaining tablespoon butter. Bake the tart for 25 to 30 minutes, until set. Remove from the oven and cool on a wire rack.

Melted Onion Tart with Parmesan

Caramelized Roasted Onions (page 130)

Pinch each of ground cumin, cayenne pepper,
ground cloves, and nutmeg

$1/4$ teaspoon salt

Half recipe Flaky Pastry (page 37)

2 eggs

2 tablespoons all-purpose flour

1 cup heavy cream or undiluted evaporated milk
(not condensed)

Freshly ground black pepper

$1/2$ cup freshly grated Parmesan

Onions, sliced and cooked in the convection oven, literally melt into sweetness. Here the melted onions are baked in a rich custard, flavored with Parmesan, and cradled in a flaky pastry. This is terrific for a special occasion. ■ Makes 8 servings

1. Position the oven racks so that they are evenly spaced, with one rack in the center of the oven. Preheat the oven to convection bake at 400°F.

2. Prepare the Caramelized Roasted Onions; remove from the oven and cool. Season with the cumin, cayenne, cloves, nutmeg, and salt.

3. Line a 9-inch pie or tart pan with the pastry, pinch the edges of the pastry to flute, line the bottom with foil, and weight down with pie weights (uncooked dried beans work well). Bake on the center rack for 15 minutes or until the edges are lightly browned. Remove from the oven; remove the pie weights (you can do this by simply lifting them in the foil out of the pan). Cool on a wire rack. Reduce the oven temperature to convection bake at 350°F.

4. Whisk the eggs in a medium bowl with the flour, cream, and black pepper until smooth. Stir in the onion mixture. Pour the custard into the pastry shell and sprinkle with the Parmesan. Bake on the center rack for 25 to 30 minutes, until the top is golden and the custard is set. Remove from the oven and cool on a wire rack.

Mozzarella Tomato Tart

Half recipe Flaky Pastry (page 37)

6 large plum (Roma) tomatoes, cut crosswise into
   $1/2$-inch slices

1 teaspoon salt

2 tablespoons Dijon mustard

3 tablespoons chopped fresh basil, or
   $1^1/2$ tablespoons dried

8 ounces fresh mozzarella, cut into $1/2$-inch slices

2 eggs

1 cup heavy cream

Freshly ground black pepper

This simple tart, a little like a quiche, is perfect as a first course or snack. Add a salad to the menu and it can star as the main dish.

■ Makes 12 first-course servings
or 8 main-dish servings

1. Roll out the pastry and fit it into the bottom and sides of an 11-inch tart pan with a removable bottom. Chill for 30 minutes

2. Sprinkle the sliced tomatoes with $1/2$ teaspoon of the salt and place them on paper towels to drain. Turn the tomatoes over and pat dry.

3. Position the oven racks so that they are evenly spaced, with one rack in the center of the oven. Preheat the oven to convection bake at 350°F. Spread the mustard on the bottom of the pastry shell and sprinkle with the basil. Distribute the tomato slices and mozzarella over the basil.

4. Mix the eggs and cream in a small bowl and season with the remaining $1/2$ teaspoon salt and the pepper. Pour the mixture evenly over the tomatoes. Bake for 25 to 30 minutes, until the custard is set. Remove from the oven and cool on a wire rack.

Roasted Vegetable Tart with Gorgonzola and Parmesan

1 pound regular or Japanese eggplant, cut into
$^1/_2$-inch cubes

2 medium portobello mushrooms, halved and cut into $^1/_4$-inch slices

1 small red onion, cut vertically into thin wedges

1 medium red bell pepper, cut into $^1/_2$-inch squares

1 medium (4 ounces) yellow squash, cut into
$^1/_2$-inch cubes

2 garlic cloves, minced

2 to 3 tablespoons olive oil

1 teaspoon kosher salt

Freshly ground black pepper

4 ounces Gorgonzola, crumbled

3 ounces cream cheese, softened

1 egg

2 tablespoons freshly grated Parmesan

Flaky Pastry (page 37)

1 tablespoon fresh rosemary leaves

1. Position the oven racks so that they are evenly spaced, with the second rack in the center of the oven. Preheat the oven to convection roast at 450°F. Cover a rimmed cookie sheet (half sheet pan) with foil and coat with nonstick spray.

2. In a large bowl, toss the eggplant, mushrooms, onion, pepper, squash, and garlic with the olive oil. Spread the vegetables on the prepared pan in an even layer and sprinkle with salt and pepper. Roast on the top rack in the oven for 15 to 20 minutes, until the vegetables are tender. Reduce the oven temperature to convection bake at 375°F.

3. Blend together the Gorgonzola, cream cheese, egg, and Parmesan in a small bowl until smooth.

4. Roll half of the pastry out to make a 14-inch round. Fit it into the bottom and sides of an 11-inch tart pan. Sprinkle with rosemary and gently press it into the dough. Spread half of the cheese mixture over the dough. Arrange the roasted vegetables on top. Top this with the egg-cheese mixture. Roll the remaining half of the pastry into a 12-inch round and fit it over the filling so it covers the pie. Brush the edges of the bottom crust with water and crimp the top and bottom edges together to seal. Pierce the top crust a few times with the tip of a knife to make steam vents. Bake the tart on the center rack of the oven until golden brown, 25 to 30 minutes. Remove from the oven and cool on a wire rack.

Cheese Soufflé

3 tablespoons butter, plus more for the dish

Freshly grated Parmesan

3 tablespoons all-purpose flour

1 cup milk

Dash cayenne pepper

$^1/_4$ teaspoon dry mustard

$^1/_2$ teaspoon salt

1 cup shredded Cheddar, Swiss, or Fontina

4 eggs, separated

Baked in the convection oven, this soufflé rises high and is almost noncollapsible. However, you'd still better have the table set and be ready to eat when the soufflé is done because it won't stay puffed forever! ■ Makes 4 servings

1. Position the oven racks so that the top rack is one level below the center of the oven. Preheat the oven to convection bake at 375°F. Butter a $1^1/_2$-quart soufflé dish and dust with Parmesan.

2. Melt the 3 tablespoons butter in a saucepan and whisk in the flour. Blend in the milk, cayenne, mustard, and salt; cook, whisking until thickened. Add the cheese and continue stirring until melted. Remove from the heat and beat in the egg yolks.

3. Whip the egg whites until they hold short, distinct peaks. Fold about half of the whites thoroughly into the sauce; gently fold in the remaining whites.

4. Pour the batter into the soufflé dish and bake for 35 minutes, until puffed and golden.

Basil and Parmesan Soufflé

In step 2, add 2 crushed garlic cloves to the butter; cook 2 to 3 minutes, until aromatic, and proceed with the directions above. Add $^1/_2$ cup prepared basil pesto and 2 tablespoons chopped fresh basil to the thickened sauce and use 1 cup freshly grated Parmesan in place of the Cheddar, Swiss, or Fontina. Finish preparing the soufflé and bake as directed.

Dilled Salmon Soufflé

3 tablespoons butter

1 tablespoon freshly grated Parmesan

4 tablespoons all-purpose flour

1 teaspoon salt

1 cup milk, heated

2 tablespoons chopped fresh flat-leaf parsley

1 teaspoon dried dill weed

1 tablespoon freshly squeezed lemon juice

4 eggs, separated

1^1/2 cups flaked, cooked salmon

Perfect for lunch or brunch, this is a classic soufflé that begins with a thick cream sauce. It bakes in the convection oven in about one-third the time of a conventional oven, although at the same temperature. ■ Makes 4 servings

1. Position the oven racks so that the top rack is one level below the center of the oven. Preheat the oven to convection bake at 350°F. Grease a 1^1/2-quart soufflé dish with 1 tablespoon of the butter and dust evenly with the Parmesan.

2. Heat the remaining 2 tablespoons butter in a 2-quart saucepan and blend in the flour and salt. Slowly whisk in the milk and heat to boiling, stirring or whisking vigorously. Cook until thickened. Remove from the heat and add the parsley, dill, and lemon juice.

3. Whisk the egg yolks and salmon into the cream sauce.

4. Whip the egg whites until they hold short, distinct peaks. Fold about half of the whites thoroughly into the sauce; gently fold in the remaining whites.

5. Pour the batter into the soufflé dish and bake for 35 minutes, until lightly browned and almost completely set in the center. Serve immediately.

Vegetable Soups

You wouldn't think that soups would benefit from convection oven cooking, but they do. Roasted vegetables take on a rich, intense flavor and can be served with a meal or snack, then turned into soup later. With tasteful seasoning and creative presentation, these soups can be not only nutritious but also low in fat and calories.

Mexican Vegetable Tortilla Soup

2 pounds (about 10) large plum (Roma) tomatoes

2 medium onions, peeled and halved (about 1 pound)

One 1^1/2-pound butternut squash, peeled, halved, seeded, and cut into ^{1}/2-inch cubes

^{3}/4 pound red-skinned potatoes, scrubbed and cut into ^{1}/2-inch cubes

1 teaspoon kosher salt

2 teaspoons olive oil

4 large garlic cloves, unpeeled

One 3-inch cinnamon stick

6 black peppercorns

1 large jalapeño

Two 5^1/2-inch corn tortillas cut in half

1 teaspoon chipotle chile powder (see Note)

1^1/2 teaspoons dried oregano

1 teaspoon ground cumin

One 15- to 16-ounce can chickpeas (garbanzo beans), undrained

^{1}/4 pound green beans, trimmed and cut into 1-inch pieces

1 cup whole corn kernels, fresh or frozen

Salt and freshly ground black pepper to taste

^{1}/3 cup chopped fresh cilantro

This updated classic soup of Mexico is easier to make when you let the convection oven do the cooking. Add a squeeze of fresh lime juice to each bowl when you serve it.

■ Makes 8 servings

1. Position the oven racks so that they are evenly spaced. Preheat the oven to convection roast at 500°F. Line two baking sheets with heavy-duty foil and coat with nonstick spray. Place the tomatoes close together on the first prepared baking sheet and fill the rest of the sheet with the onion halves. Toss the squash and potatoes with the salt and olive oil and spread them on the second baking sheet.

2. Put both sheets into the oven. Roast the onions and tomatoes for 5 minutes, then slide them into a large bowl to cool. Continue roasting the squash and potatoes for 5 more minutes, until tender, then remove them from the oven.

3. Place the garlic, cinnamon, peppercorns, and jalapeño on the same baking sheet used for the onions and tomatoes, along with the tortilla halves. Roast for 5 to 8 minutes, until the spices are fragrant and the tortillas are crisp. Remove everything to a plate.

4. Remove the skin from the tomatoes and chop the onions. Peel the garlic cloves and stem, quarter, seed, and devein the jalapeño. Put the tomatoes, onions, garlic, and jalapeño into a food processor fitted with the steel blade. Add the chipotle chile powder and process until pureed. Grind the cinnamon, peppercorns, and toasted tortillas in a spice mill or coffee grinder and add to the tomato mixture. Blend until smooth.

5. Put the puree into a large soup kettle and add the oregano, cumin, 5 cups water, the squash, potatoes, chickpeas with liquid, green beans, and corn. Cover and simmer for 15 minutes.

6. Season with salt and pepper to taste. Serve in bowls and garnish with the cilantro.

Note: Chipotle chile can be purchased as a powder or whole as dried, smoked jalapeño. To make your own chipotle chile powder, remove the seeds from the dried chile and pulverize it in a spice mill or coffee grinder.

Onion and Danish Havarti Soup

3 tablespoons butter

6 large onions, thinly sliced

$1/2$ teaspoon salt

$1^1/2$ cups white wine

8 cups chicken broth

$1/4$ teaspoon freshly ground white pepper

$1/4$ teaspoon freshly grated nutmeg

2 cups diced Danish Havarti cheese

Cooking the onions for this hearty soup requires less tending in the convection oven than in a saucepan and the aroma is just as wonderful! ■ Makes 6 servings

1. Position the oven racks so that they are evenly spaced. Preheat the oven to convection roast at 350°F. Place a heavy, shallow roasting pan in the oven and add the butter; when the butter is melted add the onions and toss to coat with the butter. Sprinkle with salt and spread the onions in an even layer.

2. Roast, uncovered, for 20 to 25 minutes, until the onions are very tender and caramelized around the edges. Stir them several times during the cooking.

3. Transfer the onions to a deep soup pot. Pour the wine into the roasting pan and scrape up the browned bits. Pour the wine into the pot with the onions and add the chicken broth, pepper, and nutmeg. Heat to a simmer and cook for 15 minutes.

4. Ladle the hot soup into bowls and top with Havarti. Serve immediately.

There are two kinds of pumpkins—those intended for carving jack-o'-lanterns, and those that are usually smaller and rounder, with thick, fleshy skins, which are intended for pumpkin pies. Either kind of pumpkin is suitable for soup, though you may need to drain the jack-o'-lantern's cooked flesh to concentrate the pulp. In the convection oven, you can roast the pumpkin to make pumpkin puree. See the Note below. ■ Makes 4 servings

Pumpkin Soup with Pecans

2 tablespoons butter

1 medium onion, finely chopped

2 cups chicken broth

2 cups roasted pumpkin puree (see Note)

$1/8$ teaspoon freshly grated nutmeg

Salt

$1/3$ cup unsweetened heavy cream, whipped, plus
    more for garnish

Toasted chopped pecans for garnish

1. Melt the butter in a small soup pot over medium heat and add the onion. Cook, stirring, until the onion is tender and translucent, 4 to 6 minutes.

2. Add the chicken broth and pumpkin puree and simmer, stirring occasionally, for 10 to 12 minutes. Put the puree in a blender and blend until smooth. Add the nutmeg and salt to taste; stir in the cream. Serve hot or chilled, topped with more cream and toasted pecans.

Note: To make roasted pumpkin puree, position the oven racks so that they are evenly spaced. Preheat the oven to convection roast at 350°F. Cover two or three shallow-rimmed baking pans or cookie sheets with foil and coat with nonstick spray. Wash 6 to 9 small pumpkins, each one no more than 6 inches in diameter. Split them and scoop out the seeds. Place them cut side down on the prepared pans. Roasting time will be about 30 minutes. Test for doneness by inserting a fork or wooden skewer into the pumpkins. When done, remove the pumpkins from the oven and cool. Scoop the flesh from the skins and puree it in a food processor fitted with the steel blade. Measure 2 cups puree and put into a heavy-duty pint-sized zip-top plastic bag, using as many bags as needed. Place the bags in the freezer one on top of the other, stacked flat. Thaw as needed. Frozen pumpkin puree will keep 3 to 4 months.

Roasted Potato and Bacon Soup

12 slices bacon

4 large baking potatoes, peeled and cut into
   $^1/_2$-inch cubes

4 green onions, chopped

8 tablespoons (1 stick) butter

$^1/_2$ cup all-purpose flour

6 cups milk, heated

1$^1/_4$ cups shredded Cheddar

1 cup sour cream

1 teaspoon salt

1 teaspoon freshly ground black pepper

This thick and creamy soup gains a rich flavor when the potatoes are roasted in a bit of bacon fat. ■ Makes 6 servings

1. Position the oven racks so that they are evenly spaced. Preheat the oven to convection roast at 450°F. Arrange the bacon slices in a shallow roasting pan and bake until crisp; remove from the oven and pour off all but 1 tablespoon of the drippings. Crumble the bacon and reserve.

2. Add the potatoes to the pan, roll them around until coated with bacon fat, and spread them in a single layer. Return the pan to the oven and roast for 20 minutes, until the potatoes are tender. Add the green onions during the last 3 minutes of roasting.

3. Heat the butter in a saucepan until melted and stir in the flour. Whisk in the milk and heat to boiling, whisking all the time. Cook until thickened.

4. Add the roasted potatoes and onions; mix in the Cheddar, sour cream, salt, and pepper. Serve with a sprinkling of bacon on top.

Roasting brings out a deep concentrated flavor in foods. This soup tastes incredibly rich, but is low in fat and calories. However, I sometimes garnish the soup with a dollop of unsweetened whipped cream. ■ Makes 4 to 6 servings

Roasted Cream of Butternut Squash Soup

One 2-pound butternut squash

1 large onion, chopped

2 garlic cloves, halved

2 tablespoons olive oil or vegetable oil

4 cups chicken broth

1 cup light cream or milk

1 teaspoon salt or to taste

Pinch cayenne pepper

1 bay leaf

Freshly squeezed lemon juice

Whipped heavy cream (unsweetened) for garnish

1. Position the oven racks so that they are evenly spaced. Preheat the oven to convection bake at 425°F. Cover two baking sheets with foil and coat lightly with nonstick spray.

2. Cut the squash in half lengthwise and remove the seeds. Place cut side down on one of the baking sheets. Combine the onion and garlic and toss with the olive oil until well coated. Spread them on the second baking sheet.

3. Place the squash on the upper rack in the oven and the onion and garlic on the rack beneath. Roast the onion and garlic for 15 to 20 minutes, until tender, and remove from the oven. Roast the squash for 25 to 30 minutes, until tender. Let cool slightly.

4. Put the onion and garlic into a food processor fitted with the steel blade or a blender. Scoop the flesh from the squash and add to the onion and garlic; process until pureed.

5. Pour the puree into a saucepan and mix in the chicken broth, cream, salt, cayenne, bay leaf, and lemon juice to taste. Simmer for 20 minutes; remove the bay leaf.

6. Serve the soup hot or chilled with a dollop of unsweetened whipped cream.

Roasted Eggplant, Zucchini, and Red Pepper Soup

2 to 3 small Japanese eggplants (about 1 pound),
   halved lengthwise

1 large sweet onion, quartered

3 tablespoons olive oil

2 medium zucchini, scrubbed and cut into 1-inch
   chunks

2 red bell peppers, cored, seeded, and quartered

2 tomatoes, cored, halved, and seeded

2 garlic cloves

1 tablespoon fresh rosemary leaves, or
   1^1/$_2$ teaspoons dried

6 cups chicken broth

Salt and freshly ground black pepper

Sour cream and store-bought pesto for garnish

Here's a soup for late summer when eggplants, tomatoes, and red peppers are luscious and ripe. Top the soup with a dollop of plain yogurt and pesto for added zip. ■ Makes about 6 servings

1. Position the oven racks so that they are evenly spaced, with one rack in the center of the oven. Preheat the oven to convection roast at 500°F. Cover a shallow 12^1/$_2$ x 17^1/$_2$-inch baking sheet with foil and coat with nonstick spray.

2. Place the eggplants, cut side up, and the onion on the baking pan. Drizzle with 2 tablespoons of the olive oil. Toss the zucchini, peppers, tomatoes, and garlic with the rosemary and the remaining 1 tablespoon olive oil and add to the baking pan. Roast the vegetables for 15 to 20 minutes or until tender.

3. Scoop out the flesh of the eggplants and put into a food processor fitted with the steel blade or a blender; discard the skin. Add the remaining vegetables and puree in batches, adding some of the chicken broth as necessary, as you go. Season with salt and pepper.

4. Put the mixture and the remaining chicken broth into a large soup pot and heat to simmering; cover and cook for 30 minutes to blend the flavors. Serve topped with sour cream and pesto.

Roasted Red Pepper Soup

6 red bell peppers

1 large sweet onion, cut into 1-inch chunks

2 garlic cloves

1 celery stalk, cut into 1-inch chunks

1 medium carrot, finely diced

1 medium red potato, scrubbed and cut into 1-inch chunks

1 tablespoon olive oil

5 cups chicken broth

Salt and freshly ground black pepper

1. Position the oven racks so they are evenly spaced. Preheat the oven to convection roast at 500°F, and roast the peppers (see page 131).

2. When the peppers are done, lower the oven temperature to 450°F. Combine the onion, garlic, celery, carrot, and potato in a large bowl. Add the olive oil and toss until the vegetables are coated. Pour the vegetables onto the foil-covered baking pan used for the peppers and spread them in an even layer.

3. Roast for 15 to 20 minutes or until the vegetables are tender and slightly browned on the edges.

Roasting red bell peppers is a snap in the convection oven because the heat can be so intense that the skin on the peppers chars without cooking the flesh. Pureed and thinned with chicken stock, they turn into a stunning and flavorful soup. ■ Makes 6 to 8 servings

4. In a food processor fitted with the steel blade or a blender, puree the vegetables with the peppers in batches, adding the chicken broth to each batch as needed. Transfer the puree to a large bowl. Add salt and pepper to taste. Serve hot or chill for at least 2 hours.

Roasted Tomato and Garlic Soup

3 pounds beefsteak or plum (Roma) tomatoes,
  preferably garden fresh

1 large sweet onion, sliced

2 garlic heads, peeled (about 20 cloves)

2 tablespoons olive oil

1 teaspoon kosher salt

1 teaspoon freshly ground black pepper

1 teaspoon dried basil

1 teaspoon dried thyme

5 cups chicken broth

Sour cream for garnish

1. Position the oven racks so that they are evenly spaced. Preheat the oven to convection roast at 450°F. Oil two large, shallow baking sheets.

2. Wash, core, and halve the tomatoes. Arrange half the tomatoes on each baking sheet and scatter the onion over them. Add the garlic and drizzle the olive oil over the vegetables. Using a spatula, turn the vegetables until they are coated with the olive oil, then spread them out in a single layer. Sprinkle with the salt and pepper.

3. Roast the vegetables for 15 to 20 minutes, until the onion begins to brown slightly.

4. Puree the roasted vegetables in a food processor fitted with the steel blade or a blender in batches, adding the basil and thyme and some of the chicken broth to each batch. Add salt and pepper to taste. Serve the soup hot or cold with a dollop of sour cream.

Roasting concentrates the flavor of tomatoes in this light, refreshing, easy-to-make soup. It's irresistible either hot or cold. ■ Makes 6 servings

Beef, Lamb, and Pork

Roasting has been the obvious selling point for convection ovens for years. Salesmen like to extol the virtues of convection roasting, even though most of us are cooking fewer large cuts of meat than ever before. Nevertheless, roasts cooked in the convection oven are a simple and dependable choice for any cook. Because larger cuts of meat are more expensive, you want to be sure that the results are tender and succulent. This is especially true when you're roasting meat for a holiday or another special occasion.

I think of roasting as falling into two categories: "slow roasting," for larger cuts of meat, and "hot roasting," for smaller cuts of meat such as chops and steaks. Either way, in the convection oven, you can add vegetables, desserts, or bread to the oven, providing that there's enough room between the racks. The roast generally cooks in the center of the oven, and accompaniments go on the rack beneath. Add them to the oven according to their cooking times.

When hot roasting small cuts, root vegetables may take a bit longer than the meat, so they should be put in the oven first. Tender vegetables such as asparagus, mushrooms, or zucchini might cook in the same time or even less than a chop or steak. Set the oven at the temperature necessary for the meat and adjust the cooking time for vegetables, as they have greater temperature flexibility.

Guidelines for Roasting Beef in a Convection Oven

Cut	Weight	Rack Position	Temperature
Rib eye roast (boneless)	3 to 8 pounds	Lower third of oven	325°F
Beef rib roast, bone in	4 to 10 pounds (2 to 5 ribs)	Lower third of oven	325°F
Tenderloin roast, trimmed	2 to 3 pounds (piece) or 4 to 5 pounds (whole)	Center	400°F
Beef round tip roast	3 to 10 pounds	Lower third of oven	300°F
Sirloin tip roast	2 to 3 pounds	Center	325°F
Chuck roast (boneless, 3 inches thick)	3 to $3^1/2$ pounds	Center	400°F
Chuck roast (bone-in, 3 inches thick)	3 to $3^1/2$ pounds (wrapped in foil)	Center	275°F (slow-roast method)
Steaks; rib eye, tenderloin, flank, Sirloin, T-bone	4 to 12 ounces, $1^1/2$ to 2 inches thick	Center	500°F

Roasting Time per Pound	Internal Temperature
Rare 15 to 23 minutes	125°F
Medium 24 to 28 minutes	135°F
Well-done 28 to 32 minutes	145°F
Rare 17 to 25 minutes	125°F
Medium 28 to 30 minutes	135°F
Well-done 30 to 32 minutes	145°F
Rare 8 to 10 minutes	125°F
Medium 10 to 15 minutes	135°F
Rare 15 to 23 minutes	140°F
Medium 24 to 28 minutes	155°F
Well-done 28 to 32 minutes	160°F
Rare 15 to 23 minutes	140°F
Medium 24 to 28 minutes	155°F
Medium-well 30 to 32 minutes	160°F
Rare 15 to 16 minutes	140°F
Medium 20 to 24 minutes	155°F
Well-done 24 to 28 minutes	160°F
Well-done 30 to 45 minutes	160°F
Rare 6 to 7 minutes	125°F
Medium 8 to 12 minutes	135°F

Tips

- Once the meat thermometer shows the desired degree of doneness, remove the roast from the oven. The final internal temperature rises 10 to 15 degrees upon standing, depending on the thickness of the roast. This is called "carryover" cooking.

- Allow the roast to stand for 10 to 15 minutes after you remove it from the oven for easier carving.

- For slow roasting, recommended for tougher cuts of meat such as bone-in chuck roast, wrap seasoned meat in foil and place on a shallow baking pan. Insert a meat thermometer or an oven probe through the foil. Allow the meat to stand for 15 minutes, wrapped, after removal from the oven.

- Roasting times are approximate because the actual time varies with the size and shape of the roast.

- For the most accurate roasting, use a meat thermometer or an oven probe, inserting it into the center of the meatiest portion, not touching bone.

- Hot-roasting time for steaks and small cuts of meat varies according to the shape of the meat.

- Hot-roasted steaks will continue to cook for about 2 minutes after being removed from the oven.

The rib eye is the prime rib of beef minus the bones. It is usually trimmed and tied. I prefer the roast taken from the small end of the loin. In the convection oven, the roast cooks in one-third to one-half the time it takes in a conventional oven. If your oven has a probe, use it for accurate timing.

■ Makes 6 to 8 servings

Roast Rib Eye of Beef with Garlic and Thyme

One 4- to 6-pound beef rib eye roast, cut from the small end of the loin and well-trimmed

2 tablespoons olive oil

4 large garlic cloves, minced

2 teaspoons dried thyme

1 teaspoon kosher salt

1^1/$_2$ teaspoons cracked black peppercorns

1. Position the oven racks so that the top rack is in the lower third of the oven. Preheat the oven to convection roast at 325°F. Coat the rack of a shallow roasting pan with nonstick spray. Place the roast, fat side up, on the rack in the pan.

2. Rub the roast with the combined olive oil, garlic, thyme, salt, and pepper. Insert the oven probe or a meat thermometer so that the tip is centered in the thickest part, not resting in fat.

3. Place the roasting pan on an oven rack in the lower third of the oven. Roast for 1^1/$_2$ to 2 hours for a medium-done 4-pound roast or until the probe or thermometer indicates the degree of doneness you prefer.

4. Remove the roast to a carving board and allow it to rest for 15 minutes before carving.

Roast Rib Eye of Beef with Root Vegetables

Prepare the roast as directed in the basic recipe. Scrub 2 pounds small red potatoes or fingerling potatoes and place them in a large bowl. Add 1 pound baby carrots to the potatoes. Cut 2 medium onions into 1-inch wedges and add to the potatoes and carrots. Drizzle with 1 tablespoon olive oil and sprinkle lightly with kosher salt and freshly ground black pepper. Put the vegetables in a shallow 15 × 10-inch jelly roll pan and bake in the oven on the rack below the roast for the last hour of roasting time or until tender. Serve the vegetables with the roast.

Classic Roast Prime Rib of Beef

**One 4- to 10-pound trimmed standing rib roast,
    chine bone removed**
1 tablespoon dried thyme, crumbled
Kosher salt
Cracked black peppercorns

1. Remove the top rack inside the oven and position it on the second rack from the bottom. Preheat the oven to convection roast at 325°F. Coat the rack of a shallow roasting pan with nonstick spray for easier cleanup.

2. Place the meat on the rack in the roasting pan and rub generously with the thyme, salt, and peppercorns. Insert the oven probe or a meat thermometer so that the tip is in the center of the muscle, not touching a bone.

3. Put the meat in the oven and roast until the probe or thermometer reaches 125°F for medium-rare. The meat continues to cook once you take it out of the oven, so be careful not to overcook it.

This is definitely a special-occasion cut of meat, but there is absolutely no better way to cook it than in the convection oven. Cooking time will be reduced by one-third to one-half to achieve the doneness you prefer. Use the probe that comes with your oven, or follow the timing and check doneness with a meat thermometer inserted into the roast or with an instant-read thermometer.

■ Makes 2 servings per pound

Roast Beef Tenderloin

One 3-pound beef tenderloin, trimmed

1 teaspoon olive oil

2 teaspoons kosher salt

3 garlic cloves, crushed

1 tablespoon dried rosemary

Roast beef tenderloin is a special-occasion meat even though it is about the simplest cut to prepare. Here's the basic method plus a wonderful variation. ■ Makes 8 servings

1. Position the oven racks so that the top rack is in the center of the oven. Preheat the oven to convection roast at 400°F. Coat the rack of a shallow roasting pan with nonstick spray.

2. Rub the beef with the olive oil and then with the salt, garlic, and rosemary. Place in the roasting pan and roast in the center of the oven for 25 to 30 minutes or until the oven probe or an instant-read thermometer registers 125°F for rare or 135°F for medium. Remove the beef from the oven and cover with a piece of foil.

3. Let the beef rest, covered, for 10 minutes before carving. The temperature will rise as the beef rests.

Roast Beef Tenderloin with Peppercorn Mustard Crust

Place 1 tablespoon each of whole black peppercorns, coriander seeds, and mustard seed in a spice grinder or coffee grinder and grind until coarse. Add 2 teaspoons kosher salt. Rub the beef with 1 teaspoon olive oil and then coat it with the spice mixture. Roast as directed above. While the beef roasts, mix 1 cup sour cream with $1/3$ cup freshly grated horseradish. Stir in 1 teaspoon kosher salt. Serve the sauce with the beef.

Chuck roast needs to be tenderized by marinating it in an acidic mixture containing lemon juice, vinegar, beer, or wine. The roast should not be cooked to well-done, as it will not be tender. Cooked in the convection oven, the roast develops a deep, rich brown on the outside while the meat inside stays tender and juicy. For this recipe to work best, be sure to select a roast that is at least 3 inches thick. ■ Makes 4 to 6 servings

Beer-Marinated Chuck Roast

One 3- to 3^1/2-pound boneless chuck roast,
   3 inches thick

1 cup beer

^{1}/2 cup vegetable oil

2 tablespoons freshly squeezed lemon juice

1 garlic clove, minced

^{3}/4 teaspoon kosher salt

^{1}/2 teaspoon freshly ground black pepper

^{1}/2 teaspoon dry mustard

2 teaspoons fresh rosemary leaves, or 1 teaspoon
   dried

^{1}/2 teaspoon dried oregano or thyme

1. Place the roast in a gallon-sized zip-top plastic bag. Add all the remaining ingredients and seal the bag. Refrigerate overnight.

2. Position the oven racks so that the top rack is in the center of the oven. Preheat the oven to convection roast at 400°F. Coat the roasting rack with nonstick spray; place the roast on the rack in a shallow roasting pan and brush with the marinade. Discard the remaining marinade.

3. Roast for 55 to 60 minutes or until the oven probe or an instant-read thermometer registers 135°F for medium rare. Remove the roast from the oven and let it rest for 10 minutes. The temperature will rise as the roast rests.

4. To carve, cut the roast diagonally across the grain.

This roast is an exception to the guidelines in the beef-roasting chart. Some butchers call this the least tender of the rounds of beef, the "knuckle cut." It needs to be cooked long and slow. When it is slow-roasted, wrapped in foil, it cooks in its own juices to tender juiciness. Normally, I would cook the roast at 250°F, but in the convection oven, I reduce the temperature to 200°F. This is a convenient way to roast an inexpensive cut of meat for a large number of people. Espresso coffee beans and a bouquet of spices contribute to the deep, rich color of the beef and the juices are transformed into a delicious mahogany-colored sauce. ■ Makes 20 to 24 servings

Espresso-Spice-Crusted Round of Beef

One 10- to 12-pound round of beef

FOR THE ESPRESSO RUB

2 tablespoons finely ground espresso coffee beans

2 tablespoons packed brown sugar

2 tablespoons kosher salt

1 tablespoon coarsely ground black pepper

1 tablespoon freshly ground black cardamom seeds (see Note)

1 tablespoon peeled and grated fresh ginger

6 garlic cloves, chopped

$^1/_4$ cup tart red currant jelly

1. Position the oven racks so that there will be adequate space for the roast; remove the top racks if necessary. Preheat the oven to convection roast at 200°F.

2. Wipe the roast dry and place it in the center of a large piece of heavy-duty foil. To make the espresso rub, combine all the ingredients and press them evenly onto the roast. Wrap the roast tightly in the foil and place in a shallow-rimmed roasting pan.

3. Roast for 6 hours or until an instant-read thermometer reaches 145°F. Remove from the oven and let stand for 15 to 20 minutes (the internal temperature will continue to rise). Meanwhile, drain the drippings into a heavy skillet and heat to boiling. Boil until the juices are thick and syrupy and reduced to about $1^1/_2$ cups. Whisk in the red currant jelly. Spoon enough sauce over the roast to glaze it.

4. To carve the roast, cut it across the grain into very thin slices (about $^1/_8$ inch thick). Spoon the remaining sauce over the slices to serve.

Note: To grind cardamom seeds, place the seeds in a spice or coffee grinder and process. Alternatively, grind using a mortar and pestle.

This is definitely a special-occasion meal, but it is so easy to do, and you can "grill" it all year round! I like to use ridged cast-iron grill pans to do everything from hamburgers to tenderloin steaks. I preheat the pan in the oven using the regular bake setting. Once it's preheated, I set the oven to convection roast or convection broil and use tongs to transfer the meat to the hot grill pan. Turn it over halfway through cooking to get grill marks on both sides. At the same time I bake thick-cut potatoes in a roasting pan on a lower oven rack. Add a simple green salad to the menu and serve with crusty bread. ■ Makes 2 servings

Oven-Grilled Beef Tenderloin Steaks with Thick-Cut Potatoes

Two 2-inch-thick beef tenderloin steaks

3 teaspoons olive oil

Kosher salt

Cracked black peppercorns

2 large baking potatoes, scrubbed

1. Position the oven racks so that the top rack is 5 or 6 inches from the top of the oven. Place a ridged cast-iron grill pan on the top rack of the oven and preheat the oven to 500°F. Once preheated, set the oven to convection roast or convection broil at 500°F.

2. Meanwhile, rub the steaks with 2 teaspoons of the olive oil and sprinkle with salt and pepper to taste. Set aside.

3. Cut each potato into 6 lengthwise wedges. Toss with the remaining 1 teaspoon olive oil and salt to taste. Coat a shallow-rimmed pan with a nonstick spray and add the potatoes in a single layer. Put into the oven on the lowest rack. Bake the potatoes for 5 minutes before adding the steaks.

4. Using tongs, transfer the steaks to the hot grill pan. Roast for 5 minutes, turn them over, and cook them until done to your liking or until an instant-read thermometer registers 125°F for rare or 135°F for medium. The steaks will continue to cook after you take them out of the oven.

5. Remove the steaks from the oven to warm plates, and let them rest for 5 minutes. Check the potatoes with a fork for doneness. They should take about 15 minutes. Remove the potatoes from the oven and serve with the steaks.

Garlic-Roasted Beef Sirloin Steaks with Asparagus and Hot Tomato Salad

Four 1¹/4-inch-thick sirloin steaks

¹/3 cup extra virgin olive oil

2 large garlic cloves, minced

2 tablespoons chopped fresh rosemary, or
    1 tablespoon dried, crushed

12 to 16 thick asparagus spears, trimmed

6 to 8 paper-thin slices prosciutto, cut in half
    lengthwise

4 plum (Roma) tomatoes, quartered

8 medium cremini mushrooms or small portobello
    mushrooms, halved

1 teaspoon kosher salt

¹/2 teaspoon cracked black peppercorns

1. Position the oven racks so that the top rack is 5 or 6 inches from the top of the oven. Place a ridged cast-iron grill pan on the top rack of the oven and preheat the oven to 500°F. Once pre-heated, set the oven to convection roast or convection broil at 500°F. Cover a shallow baking pan with foil and coat with nonstick spray for cooking the vegetables.

2. Combine the olive oil, garlic, and rosemary and brush the steaks with this mixture. Set aside.

3. Wrap the asparagus spears with the pro-sciutto and place them on the foil-covered baking pan. Brush them with some of the olive oil mixture.

4. Toss the tomatoes and mushrooms with enough of the olive oil mixture to coat all the pieces lightly and put them on the baking sheet with the asparagus. Drizzle the remaining olive oil mixture over all the vegetables and sprinkle with salt and pepper. Place the pan in the center of the oven and roast for 10 minutes.

5. Add the steaks to the preheated grill pan on the top rack of the oven. After 3 to 5 minutes turn the steaks and cook to your preferred doneness, 3 to 5 minutes longer. Remove the vegetables to a warm serving platter and cook the steaks until done to your liking.

6. Let the steaks rest for 5 minutes before carving. With a sharp knife, cut the steaks diagonally into thin slices.

Here's a quick hot-roasted meal that's as ideal for entertaining as it is for a busy weekday. All you need to add are some tossed greens and crusty bread. ■ Makes 4 servings

Oven-Grilled Teriyaki Flank Steak

One 1³/4- to 2-pound flank steak
1/2 cup soy sauce
1/4 cup sake or dry sherry
1/4 cup honey
2 tablespoons vegetable oil
1 garlic clove, minced
1 teaspoon peeled and grated fresh ginger, or
   1/2 teaspoon ground
1/4 teaspoon freshly ground black pepper

1. Wipe the meat dry and place it in a large, heavy duty zip-top plastic bag.

2. Combine the remaining ingredients and pour them into the bag with the meat. Close and marinate in the refrigerator for at least 3 hours or overnight.

3. Position the oven racks so that the top rack is 5 or 6 inches from the top of the oven. Place a ridged cast-iron grill pan on the top rack of the oven and preheat the oven to 500°F. Once preheated, set the oven to convection roast or convection broil at 500°F.

4. Using long tongs, remove the meat from the marinade and place it on the preheated pan. Discard the marinade. Convection roast for 5 minutes; turn over and cook for 5 more minutes for rare, 7 more minutes for medium, and 10 more minutes for well-done.

5. Place the meat on a carving board, cover, and let it rest for 5 to 10 minutes. Use a sharp knife to cut it diagonally into thin slices.

I love to grill flank steak outdoors, but sometimes it isn't possible. The convection oven is a wonderful substitute. If you have a cast-iron grill pan long enough to accommodate a flank steak, place it in the oven when you begin to preheat it. Otherwise, use the roasting pan and rack assembly that comes with your oven. I recommend preheating the oven for at least 10 minutes.

■ Makes 6 servings

Meatballs baked in the convection oven are cooked as quickly as a pan of cookies—no greasy smells or mess. I bake meatballs for kids this way. This isn't a fancy meal—just serve them over mashed potatoes, or in a bun or a wrap. ■ Makes 8 servings

Baked Meatballs

1 pound lean ground pork

1 pound ground beef round

1^1/2 cups finely chopped onions

1 cup fine dried bread crumbs

1 cup milk, water, or chicken broth

3 eggs, lightly beaten

1 cup finely minced fresh parsley

1 teaspoon dried thyme

1 teaspoon kosher salt

^{1}/2 teaspoon freshly ground black pepper

1. Position the oven racks so that one rack is in the center of the oven. Preheat the oven to convection roast at 400°F. Cover a large, shallow baking pan with foil and coat with nonstick spray.

2. In a large mixing bowl, combine all the ingredients together until well mixed. With a medium ice cream scoop, shape the meatballs and place them close together on the baking pan.

3. Place the pan in the center of the oven and roast for 10 minutes, until the meatballs are cooked through and browned. To check for doneness, cut one meatball in half—it should be juicy and pinkish. Remove from the oven and serve.

Old-Fashioned Meat Loaf

1 pound lean ground pork

1 pound ground beef round

1 1/2 cups finely chopped onions

1 cup fresh bread crumbs

1 cup tomato sauce or chopped fresh tomatoes

3 eggs, lightly beaten

1 teaspoon kosher salt

1/2 teaspoon freshly ground black pepper

1. Position the oven racks so that one rack is in the center of the oven. Preheat the oven to convection bake at 350°F. Lightly grease a 9 × 5-inch loaf pan.

2. In a large mixing bowl, combine all the ingredients together until well mixed.

3. Turn the mixture into the loaf pan and mound the top slightly. Insert the oven probe into the center of the loaf if desired, and set to 160°F.

4. Bake in the center of the oven until the temperature reaches 160°F in the center of the meat loaf, about 55 minutes. To check, insert an instant-read thermometer into the center of the loaf after 50 minutes and check the temperature. Remove the thermometer if you need to return the loaf to the oven.

This is the grandmother of all meat loaf, especially juicy when cooked in a loaf pan. It also can be baked free form— just shape the meat mixture into an oblong loaf and set it on a rimmed baking pan. Either way, the cooking time is reduced in the convection oven. Serve slices of this everyday favorite with mashed potatoes and a salad. Leftovers make great sandwiches. You might bake some vegetables or biscuits along with the meat loaf, either on the rack above or below, while it cooks.

■ Makes 8 servings

5. Remove the pan from the oven, pour off the excess fat, and let the meat loaf stand for 15 minutes before serving.

Guidelines for Roasting Lamb in a Convection Oven

Cut	Weight	Rack Position	Temperature
Leg of lamb, bone in	5 to 10 pounds	Center	325°F
Leg of lamb, boneless	$3^1/2$ to 5 pounds	Center (use oven probe)	325°F
Leg of lamb, boneless, hot-roast method	$3^1/2$ to 5 pounds	Center (use oven probe)	425°F for 20 minutes, then reduce temperature to 350°F until desired internal temperature is reached
Rack of lamb, hot-roast method	$1^1/2$ pounds	Center and on roasting rack	500°F
Lamb chops	1" to $1^1/2$" thick	Top rack	500°F

Roasting Time per Pound	Internal Temperature
Rare 8 to 11 minutes	130°F
Medium 8 to 11 minutes	140°F
Well-done 12 to 20 minutes	160° to 170°F
Rare 15 to 17 minutes	130°F
Medium 17 to 20 minutes	140°F
Well-done 20 to 24 minutes	160° to 170°F
Approximately 50 minutes total roasting time, until meat thermometer registers doneness desired. Add 30 to 35 minutes for well-done.	Rare 130°F Medium 140°F Well-done 160° to 170°F
Roast 5 minutes for rare, 8 minutes for medium-rare. Turn over and continue roasting for 5 to 8 minutes. Let rest for 10 minutes after roasting	Rare 130°F Medium 140°F Well-done 160° to 170°F
Roast 5 minutes on one side. Turn over and roast 3 to 5 minutes longer until done to your liking.	

Leg of lamb is a traditional Easter and Passover dish, but it makes a wonderful company meal any time. ■ Makes 10 to 12 servings

Roast Leg of Lamb

One 5- to 10-pound bone-in leg of lamb
4 garlic cloves, sliced
1 tablespoon paprika
1 1/2 teaspoons dried rosemary
2 teaspoons kosher salt
1/2 teaspoon freshly ground black pepper

1. Position the oven racks so that the top rack is in the center of the oven. Preheat the oven to convection roast at 325°F. Cut slits in the fat cover of the lamb with a knife. Push slices of garlic into the cuts as deeply as possible. Combine the paprika, rosemary, salt, and pepper and rub the lamb all over with the mixture.

2. Coat a rack with nonstick spray and place over a shallow, open roasting pan. Place the lamb, fat side up, on the rack.

3. Roast the lamb in the center of the oven for 8 to 11 minutes per pound or until an instant-read thermometer registers 130°F for rare, 140°F for medium, or 160° to 170°F for well-done. Remove the lamb from the oven, cover with foil, and let it rest for 15 minutes, during which time the internal temperature will rise by 5°F.

Leg of Lamb with Jalapeño and Garlic Marinade

Combine 12 garlic cloves, 1 to 4 seeded jalapeños, 1/2 cup freshly squeezed lemon juice, 2 tablespoons Dijon mustard, 2 teaspoons kosher salt, and 2 teaspoons freshly ground black pepper in a blender or the bowl of a food processor fitted with the steel blade and process until smooth. Rub the lamb with this mixture and marinate in the refrigerator for 2 hours. Continue from step 2 above.

Marinated Leg of Lamb with Peppercorn Crust

Combine 1 tablespoon crushed multicolored peppercorns, 1 tablespoon crushed dried rosemary, 1/2 cup fresh mint leaves, 5 crushed garlic cloves, 1/2 cup red wine vinegar, 1/4 cup soy sauce, and 1/2 cup dry red wine. Place the leg of lamb in a large nonreactive container and pour the mixture over it. Refrigerate for at least 8 hours, turning the meat two or three times. Remove it from the marinade and spread with 2 to 4 tablespoons Dijon mustard and pat 2 tablespoons crushed multicolored peppercorns into the mustard. Continue from step 2 above.

Boneless Leg of Lamb with Garlic and Rosemary

One 3^1/$_2$- to 4-pound boneless leg of lamb
1 tablespoon Dijon mustard
2 garlic cloves, minced
1 tablespoon dried rosemary
1 tablespoon olive oil

1. Position the oven racks so that there is one rack in the center of the oven. Preheat the oven to convection roast at 425°F.

2. Stir together the mustard, garlic, rosemary, and olive oil to make a paste and spread it evenly over the lamb. Insert the oven probe or a meat thermometer into the center of the lamb.

3. Roast the lamb in the center of the oven for 20 minutes at 425°F. Reduce the temperature to convection roast at 350°F and roast for 30 more minutes or until the temperature reaches 130°F for rare, 140°F for medium-rare, or 160° to 170°F for well-done.

4. Remove the lamb from the oven; cover with foil, and let it rest for 10 minutes before carving.

Boneless leg of lamb is versatile and easy to prepare. One of my favorite and easiest rubs for lamb combines the flavors of garlic and rosemary.

■ Makes 6 to 8 servings

Have the butcher trim (french) the rib bones. In the convection oven, the cooking time is cut by about half, and the lamb turns out beautifully browned and very juicy. When still pink, it is the juiciest. It is best to marinate the lamb for at least an hour or even overnight. ■ Makes 4 servings

Rack of Lamb with Mustard Crust

2 racks of lamb, 8 ribs per rack, trimmed and fat
   removed (about 1^1/2 pounds total)
^{1}/2 cup Dijon mustard
2 tablespoons soy sauce
1 teaspoon dried rosemary
2 large garlic cloves, minced
2 tablespoons olive oil

1. Pat the lamb dry with paper towels. Combine all the remaining ingredients in a zip-top plastic bag; add the lamb, seal the bag, and knead it around the lamb to work in the marinade and coat the meat thoroughly. Let it sit at room temperature for an hour or refrigerate overnight. If refrigerating overnight, bring to room temperature before roasting; this takes about 2 hours.

2. Position the oven racks so that the top rack is 6 inches below the top of the oven. Preheat the oven to convection roast at 500°F. Coat the meat roasting rack that comes with your oven with nonstick spray for easier cleanup. Set the rack over its pan.

3. Remove the meat from the marinade, leaving a coating on the meat. Discard the bag and the rest of the marinade. Place the lamb on the roasting rack, fat side up, place on the top oven rack, and roast for 5 minutes for rare or 8 minutes for medium-rare. Turn the lamb over and continue roasting for 5 more minutes for rare and 8 minutes for medium-rare. Remove the lamb from the oven, cover it with foil, and let it rest for 10 minutes before carving.

4. Cut between the bones of the rack and serve the lamb in 1-rib pieces.

Lemon Pepper–Marinated Lamb Chops

12 thick-cut rib lamb chops

2 tablespoons olive oil

2 garlic cloves, minced

2 tablespoons lemon pepper seasoning, or

> **1 tablespoon freshly grated lemon zest and**

> **1 tablespoon coarsely ground black pepper**

1. Rub the lamb chops with the olive oil and garlic and sprinkle with the lemon pepper seasoning. Let the chops stand for 1 hour, or cover and allow to marinate in the refrigerator overnight.

2. Position the oven racks so that the top rack is about 6 inches from the top of the oven. Pre-heat the oven to convection roast at 500°F. Lightly oil a roasting rack set over a shallow roasting pan, or cover a shallow-rimmed cookie sheet with foil and coat with nonstick spray.

3. Place the chops on the prepared rack or pan. Roast them in the upper third of the oven for 5 minutes; turn the chops over and continue roasting for 3 to 5 more minutes or until done to your liking.

So simple, yet so flavorful. These lamb chops roast to medium-rare in 8 to 10 minutes in the convection oven. Lamb chops are difficult to probe with a thermometer because they are so small. You can cut one to determine doneness.

■ Makes 6 servings, 2 chops each

Guidelines for Roasting Pork in a Convection Oven

Cut	Weight	Rack Position	Temperature
Roast leg of pork (butt)	4 to 6 pounds	Lower third of oven	325°F
Shoulder blade roast	4 to 6 pounds	Lower third of oven	325°F
Pork loin, boneless	3 to 4 pounds	Lower third of oven	325°F
Crown roast of pork	6 to 10 pounds	Lower third of oven	325°F
Pork loin, bone-in	3 to 4 pounds	Lower third of oven	325°F
Boneless pork tenderloins	$3/4$ to 1 pound	Center or top	425°F
Fully cooked ham	4 to 10 pounds	Lower third of oven	300°F convection bake
Bone-in ribs (spareribs)	2 to 6 pounds	Center	400°F convection roast
Boneless pork loin ribs (spareribs)	2 to 6 pounds	Center	400°F convection roast
Boneless pork chops	1″ to $1^1/2$″ thick	Top	475°F convection roast

Roasting Time per Pound	Internal Temperature
30 to 35 minutes	170°F
25 to 35 minutes	160° to 170°F
18 to 22 minutes	160°F
18 to 20 minutes	160°F
18 to 20 minutes	160°F
10 to 12 minutes	160°F
15 to 18 minutes	150°F
30 to 35 minutes total	NA
25 to 30 minutes total	NA
14 to 16 minutes total	160°F

Tips:

- After removing the meat from the oven, the final internal temperature rises 10 to 15 degrees, depending on the thickness of the roast.
- Roasting times are approximate because the actual time varies with the size and shape of the roast.
- Roasting times are for meat taken directly from the refrigerator.
- Use the probe that comes with your oven for the most accurate roasting, inserting it into the center of the meatiest portion, not touching the bone. Otherwise, use an instant-read thermometer, inserted into the meatiest portion of the meat, but do not place the thermometer into the oven if it has a plastic casing.
- If you use a moist, sweet glaze for ham or pork roasts, brush it on during the last 5 to 10 minutes of roasting to prevent burning.

This treatment is a great way to dress up a precooked smoked ham for a holiday table. ■ Makes 16 servings

Baked Ham with Mustard and Brown Sugar Crust

One 4- to 5-pound boneless ham, fully cooked
$1/2$ to 1 cup Dijon mustard
2 cups fine dried bread crumbs
1 cup packed brown sugar
2 teaspoons ground ginger

1. Position the oven racks so that the top rack is 4 to 5 inches below the center of the oven. Pre-heat the oven to convection bake at 300°F. Coat a shallow roasting pan with nonstick cooking spray and place the ham in the pan.

2. Place the pan on the top rack and bake for 1 hour. Take the ham out of the oven and smear it with a generous coating of mustard. Mix the bread crumbs, brown sugar, and ginger together and pat a generous coating evenly over the whole ham.

3. Return the ham to the oven and bake for about 30 minutes or until thoroughly heated.

Ham with Ancho-Honey Mustard Glaze

Bake the ham for $1^1/2$ hours at 300°F, then coat with a mixture of 1 cup honey, $1/4$ cup Dijon mustard, and 2 teaspoons ground ancho chile powder (see page 206), and continue baking for 5 to 10 more minutes, until the glaze is shiny.

Chili-Spiced Boneless Pork Ribs

2 pounds thick-cut boneless pork loin ribs
   (8 pieces)
1 tablespoon chili powder or coarsely ground black
   pepper
1 teaspoon kosher salt
All-purpose flour

FOR THE SAUCE

4 tablespoons ($1/2$ stick) butter
$1/4$ cup freshly squeezed lemon juice
$1/4$ cup chili powder
2 tablespoons dry mustard
1 tablespoon sugar
1 tablespoon paprika
1 teaspoon onion powder
1 teaspoon garlic powder
$1/2$ teaspoon salt

Today's low-fat pork is easily overcooked, making it tough and dry. In the past, pork shoulder ribs were thought to require hours of cooking. Not true. Just try this method. While the ribs cook in a hot oven, combine the sauce ingredients and brush the meat generously with it during the final few minutes of cooking.

■ Makes 4 servings

1. Position the oven racks so that the top rack is about 8 inches from the top of the oven. Preheat the oven to convection roast at 400°F. Assemble the broiler pan and rack that comes with your oven and lightly grease the rack. Or, cover a shallow baking pan or broiler pan with foil and coat with nonstick spray.

2. Sprinkle the ribs with the chili powder and salt, then dust lightly with the flour. Arrange the rib pieces 2 inches apart on the prepared pan and convection roast on the top rack for 20 minutes.

3. To make the sauce, combine all the ingredients with 1 cup water in a medium saucepan, mix well, and bring to a boil. Reduce the heat and simmer for 10 minutes. Brush the sauce on the ribs and roast for 10 to 15 more minutes. Remove from the oven and serve with additional sauce.   (continued)

Spice-Rubbed Boneless Pork Ribs with Honey and Mustard

Combine 2 minced garlic cloves with 1 teaspoon crushed dried rosemary, 1 teaspoon crumbled dried sage, 1 teaspoon crumbled dried thyme, 1 teaspoon kosher salt, and $1/2$ teaspoon coarsely ground black pepper. Rub the ribs with 1 tablespoon olive oil and then with the herb mixture. Place on the prepared pan and roast as described above. While the ribs are roasting, combine $1/3$ cup honey and $1/3$ cup Dijon mustard with 1 tablespoon freshly squeezed lemon juice. Brush the ribs with the honey mixture during the last 5 minutes of roasting.

This is a festive roast for a holiday meal. Ask the butcher to prepare it so the chops can be cut into serving portions easily. Allow one to two chops per adult serving. Because the crown roast of pork is a very lean cut, it should be cooked to 160°F. It has a tendency to be oval rather than round because it is made from two pork loins trimmed and tied together. To improve the shape, I place a lightly oiled, heatproof glass jelly jar down into the center (described in step 3).

■ Makes about 8 servings

Crown Roast of Pork

One 7- to 8-pound crown roast of pork

FOR THE SEASONING MIXTURE

1 tablespoon lemon pepper seasoning, or

   1¹/₂ teaspoons freshly grated lemon zest and

   1¹/₂ teaspoons coarsely ground black pepper

1 loosely packed tablespoon each of dried

   rosemary, dried thyme, dried sage

1 bay leaf

1 garlic clove

1. Position the oven racks so that the top rack is 3 inches below the center of the oven. Preheat the oven to convection roast at 325°F. Assemble the roasting pan and rack that comes with the oven and coat the rack with nonstick spray.

2. Place the roast on the rack over the roasting pan. To make the seasoning mixture, combine the lemon pepper with the rosemary, thyme, sage, bay leaf, and garlic in a spice mill or coffee grinder and process until the mixture is smooth. Rub the seasoning mixture on the roast.

3. Pull open the center of the roast and place a lightly oiled, heatproof 8-ounce glass jelly jar down into the center to give the roast a round shape. Cut small pieces of foil and cover the tips of the bones so they don't burn while roasting.

4. Insert the oven probe or meat thermometer into the center of the meaty portion of the roast. Place in the oven on the top rack and attach the probe to the receptacle in the oven wall. Set the probe temperature at 160°F. Roast for 18 to 20 minutes per pound, or until the oven probe or meat thermometer reaches 160°F.

5. When the roast is done, remove it from the oven and place on a warm serving platter; cover it loosely with foil and let rest for 10 to 15 minutes. Using a pair of tongs, loosen the jelly jar and remove it from the center of the roast.

Dry-Roasted Baby Back Ribs

4 pounds baby back ribs, cut into 6 equal pieces

3 tablespoons olive oil

3 garlic cloves, minced

2 tablespoons lemon pepper seasoning, or

    1 tablespoon freshly grated lemon zest and

    1 tablespoon coarsely ground black pepper

1 tablespoon paprika

1 teaspoon coarsely ground black pepper

These ribs are rubbed with an oil and spice mixture. They cook to tender perfection in less than an hour in the convection oven.

■ Makes 6 servings

1. Position the oven racks so that they are evenly spaced. Preheat the oven to convection roast at 400°F.

2. Pat the ribs dry. Combine the olive oil, garlic, lemon pepper, paprika, and black pepper and rub the mixture over the ribs on all sides. Place the ribs, bone side up, on the roasting rack placed over the roasting pan that comes with your oven. For easiest cleanup, the rack should be coated with nonstick spray.

3. Roast in the center of the oven for 20 minutes; turn the ribs over. Roast for 10 to 15 more minutes, until the ribs are browned. Remove the ribs from the oven and transfer them to a serving platter.

Spareribs with Garlic and Rosemary

Rub the ribs with 4 minced garlic cloves; 2 tablespoons olive oil; 2 tablespoons crushed, dried rosemary; and 2 teaspoons kosher salt. Roast as directed above.

Oven-Barbecued Spareribs

4 pounds pork spareribs, cut into 3-rib pieces

1 medium onion, chopped

1 red bell pepper, seeded and chopped

4 garlic cloves, minced

1 medium tomato, chopped, or $1/2$ cup ketchup or tomato sauce

$1/2$ cup firmly packed brown sugar

$1/4$ cup light molasses

$1/4$ cup soy sauce

1 teaspoon brown or Dijon mustard

$1/2$ teaspoon sesame oil

Dash hot sauce

1. Position the oven racks so that they are evenly spaced. Preheat the oven to convection bake at 400°F. Cover one or two shallow-rimmed baking pans with foil and coat with nonstick spray.

2. Arrange the spareribs on the baking pan or pans, bone side up. Place in the oven. If using one pan, place it in the center of the oven. If using two pans, place them so that one is in the upper two-thirds and the other in the bottom two-thirds of the oven.

3. Bake for 20 minutes, turn the ribs over, and bake for 10 more minutes.

4. Meanwhile, combine all the remaining ingredients in the bowl of a food processor fitted with the steel blade. Process just until all the ingredients are minced (not pureed).

5. Pour the sauce over the ribs, meaty sides up. Reduce the oven temperature to 350°F and continue baking for 25 to 30 more minutes, until the ribs are glazed.

Asian-Style Barbecued Ribs

Convection bake the spareribs as directed above. While the ribs bake, combine 4 large minced garlic cloves, 1 tablespoon peeled and minced fresh ginger, $2/3$ cup soy sauce, $2/3$ cup hoisin sauce, $1/4$ cup honey, 3 tablespoons ketchup, 3 tablespoons cider vinegar, 3 tablespoons dry sherry, and 1 teaspoon red pepper flakes. In step 5 above, baste the ribs with this sauce and cook as directed.

You can precook spareribs without covering them using this easy convection oven method. While the ribs are in their first stage of cooking, make the barbecue sauce for the final glazing and baking, or use your favorite store-bought brand. ■ Makes 6 servings

Pork loin is one of my favorite meats to convection roast because it's readily available and easy to handle, requiring no special trimming or cutting. If you simply season it with salt and pepper and use the same temperature and timing as with this recipe, the meat is tender and delicious. Most ovens come with a probe. When you're roasting pork loin it's best to use it, so that you don't accidentally overcook the meat, making it dry rather than succulent and juicy. Set the probe to 160°F. The roast continues to cook for a few minutes once you've removed it from the oven. When you convection roast the pork, it is done in one-third to one-half the usual time. ■ Makes 6 servings

Glazed Pork Loin with Honey and Mustard

One 4-pound boneless center-cut pork loin

2 garlic cloves, minced

1 teaspoon minced fresh rosemary, or $^1/_2$ teaspoon dried, crumbled

1 teaspoon minced fresh sage, or $^1/_2$ teaspoon dried, crumbled

1 teaspoon minced fresh thyme, or $^1/_2$ teaspoon dried

1 tablespoon kosher salt

1 teaspoon coarsely ground black pepper

FOR THE GLAZE

$^1/_2$ cup honey

$^1/_4$ cup Dijon mustard

1 tablespoon freshly squeezed lemon juice

1. Position the oven racks so that the top rack is in the center of the oven. Preheat the oven to convection roast at 325°F.

2. Pat the pork dry with paper towels. Coat the rack and a shallow roasting pan with nonstick spray. Place the pork on the rack over the pan.

3. Combine the garlic, rosemary, sage, thyme, salt, and pepper in a small bowl. Rub the mixture all over the pork.

4. Roast the pork on the top rack for 18 to 22 minutes per pound or until the oven probe or a meat thermometer reaches 160°F. To make the glaze, mix the honey, mustard, and lemon juice together and brush the mixture over the pork during the last 15 minutes of roasting.

5. Remove the pork from the oven and cover with foil. Let it rest for 10 to 15 minutes before carving.

You need a V-shaped roasting rack for this. The pork is cooked to "tender rags"—long and slow with air circulating around it—producing the effect of rotisserie cooking. For a Caribbean flair, serve with black beans and rice. Serve leftovers in sandwiches. ■ Makes 6 to 8 servings

Orange-Marinated Pork Roast

One 5- to 7-pound boneless pork shoulder
    roast, tied

1 cup freshly squeezed orange juice

2 tablespoons olive oil

3 garlic cloves, minced

1 medium onion, finely chopped

1 teaspoon dried oregano

1 teaspoon dried sage

1 bay leaf, crumbled

1 teaspoon kosher salt

1/2 teaspoon freshly ground black pepper

1. Place the roast into a zip-top plastic bag. Add the remaining ingredients. Close the bag and gently knead it to mix the contents. Refrigerate overnight.

2. Position the oven racks so that the top rack is in the center of the oven. Preheat the oven to convection roast at 275°F. Place the pork on a rack over a shallow roasting pan. Remove the roast from the marinade; save the marinade. Place the roast on the rack and insert the oven probe or a meat thermometer into the meatiest part.

3. Roast for 4 hours, basting occasionally with the remaining marinade, until the meat reaches 160°F.

4. Remove the meat from the rack. Let it rest for 15 minutes before carving.

Oven-Grilled Boneless Pork Chops

6 boneless pork loin chops, 1^1/4 to 1^1/2 inches thick
1 to 2 tablespoons olive oil or vegetable oil
1 to 2 tablespoons Cajun spice mix, lemon pepper
   seasoning, or other spice mix for pork

1. Place a ridged cast-iron grill pan on the center rack of the oven. Preheat the oven to convection roast at 475°F.

2. Brush the pork chops with the olive oil and sprinkle the spice mix evenly on both sides of each chop. Place the seasoned pork chops on the preheated grill pan.

3. Cook for 7 minutes, turn over, and cook for 7 to 8 more minutes. To check for doneness, remove one chop from the oven and insert an instant-read thermometer into the center from the side. Cooking time will vary depending on the thickness of the chops. For the juiciest results, do not exceed 160°F.

4. Remove the chops from the oven and serve.

This is a simple and tasty way to grill boneless pork chops, and you can roast vegetables at the same time by placing them in a pan on the rack beneath the meat.

■ Makes 6 servings

Roasted Pork Tenderloins

2 pork tenderloins (about 3 pounds total)
1 tablespoon olive oil or vegetable oil
2 teaspoons kosher salt
1 teaspoon coarsely ground black pepper

1. Position the oven racks so that the top rack is about 6 inches from the top of the oven. Preheat the oven to convection roast at 425°F. Rub the tenderloins with the olive oil, salt, and pepper. Arrange them at least 3 inches apart on the roasting rack that comes with the oven.

2. Roast the tenderloins on the top rack for 25 minutes or until an instant-read thermometer registers 160°F.

3. Transfer the tenderloins to a cutting board and let them rest, covered with foil, for 5 minutes. Cut into crosswise diagonal slices.

Lemon Pepper Pork Tenderloins

Rub the tenderloins with olive oil and then with 1 tablespoon lemon pepper seasoning. Roast as directed above.

Pork Tenderloins with Hoisin, Ginger, and Five-Spice Powder

Place the tenderloins in a large, heavy-duty zip-top plastic bag. Add 3 minced garlic cloves, 1 cup soy sauce, $1/2$ cup hoisin sauce, 2 tablespoons honey, 2 tablespoons ketchup, 2 tablespoons cider vinegar, 2 tablespoons dry sherry, and 1 teaspoon five-spice powder. Seal the bag and knead it so that the pork and marinade are evenly distributed. Refrigerate for at least 3 hours or overnight. Remove the tenderloins from the marinade and roast as directed above, basting twice.

Tender, juicy pork tenderloins cook as quickly as boneless chicken breasts.

■ Makes 6 servings

Poultry

The Guidelines for Roasting Poultry chart (page 92) offers a quick time and temperature reference. There is a slight difference in timing depending on how chilled the bird is when it goes into the oven.

Although I prefer to roast whole birds unstuffed, the general rule of thumb is to add 4 minutes per pound to the total roasting time when stuffed. Here are some rules if you do decide to stuff a turkey or chicken:

- Stuff the bird just before roasting and never ahead of time, which would give any harmful bacteria time to grow.
- Have the stuffing hot and pack it loosely into the cavity. The stuffing must reach 160°F during roasting to be sure any harmful bacteria are killed. If the stuffing is cold, it may not reach this temperature at all.
- When the bird is cooked, plunge an instant-read thermometer into the body cavity. If the bird is done but the stuffing has still not reached 160°F, remove the bird from the oven and scoop out the stuffing into a baking pan. Bake the stuffing while the bird rests before carving.
- Always remove all the stuffing from the bird because it may stay warm for several hours even if the bird is refrigerated.

CHECKING FOR DONENESS Many recipes will say to cook until the "juices run clear." But, truthfully, it is not easy to check for doneness accurately unless you use an instant-read thermometer. Chicken and turkey breast meat is done when the thermometer registers 160°F. However, that doesn't mean the leg is fully cooked, especially the inner thigh. To check the leg, stick the stem of the thermometer into the thickest part of the inner thigh without touching the bone. The leg is done at 170°F. If you want to avoid a pinkish color, the thermometer should reach 180°F; however, you risk drying out the breast meat. Luckily, when cooked in a convection oven, poultry stays moist longer because juices are sealed in the breast meat early during the cooking process.

Follow the time and temperature guidelines given in the chart. After numerous tests, I offer two basic methods for roasting a whole chicken. Each has an advantage.

In Method One, the roasting starts out at a high temperature (450°F), which is then reduced (to 300°F), producing a nicely browned, evenly cooked, and very juicy roast chicken. In Method Two, the chicken is roasted at a steady temperature of 350°F with excellent results. The advantage here is that you just put the chicken into the oven and forget it. Method Two may result in a slightly longer cooking time for the inner thigh to reach the desired temperature.

Skinless, boneless chicken breasts are one of the most readily available, versatile, quick-to-prepare, and popular meats. Though the variations are almost limitless, here are six different recipes that work particularly well in the convection oven—recipes to consider for both family and guests. Use them as a guide for your favorite chicken breast recipes.

Skinless, boneless chicken breast halves are usually sold in packages that contain 4 pieces and weigh between $1^1/4$ pounds and $1^1/2$ pounds. A little more or a little less isn't going to make a huge difference in cooking time. Just be sure not to overcook chicken breasts, as they are very lean and toughen when overcooked.

Guidelines for Roasting Poultry in a Convection Oven

Poultry	Weight	Rack Position	Temperature
Whole broiler-fryer chicken	3 to 4 pounds	Center	450°F, then 300°F
Whole roasting chicken	4$\frac{1}{2}$ to 6$\frac{1}{2}$ pounds	Center	325°F
Chicken quarters	3 pounds	Center	425°F
Chicken pieces	3 pounds	Center	425°F
Turkey, unstuffed	8 to 14 pounds 14 to 18 pounds 18 to 24 pounds	Lower third of oven Lower third of oven Lower third of oven	325°F 300°F 300°F
Turkey breast, boneless	4 to 6 pounds	Center	325°F
Cornish game hens, stuffed	$\frac{3}{4}$ pound to 2 pounds	Center	350°F
Cornish game hens, unstuffed	$\frac{3}{4}$ pound to 2 pounds	Center	350°F
Duck	4 to 5 pounds	Center	325°F
Goose	8 to 10 pounds	Lower third of oven	325°F

Roasting Time	Internal Temperature
15 to 20 minutes (reduce temperature after 25 minutes) per pound	170° to 175°F (inner thigh)
20 to 24 minutes per pound	170° to 175°F (inner thigh)
25 to 30 minutes total	170°F or until juices run clear
25 to 30 minutes total	170°F or until juices run clear
8 to 11 minutes per pound	170° to 175°F (inner thigh)
8 to 11 minutes per pound	170° to 175°F (inner thigh)
9 to 10 minutes per pound	170° to 175°F (inner thigh)
16 to 19 minutes per pound	165° to 170°F
50 to 55 minutes total	170° to 175°F (inner thigh)
40 to 50 minutes total	170° to 175°F (inner thigh)
24 to 26 minutes per pound	180°F
24 to 26 minutes per pound	180°F

Roast chicken is a simple but perfect dish when convection roasted: the meat is juicy and the skin is brown and crisp. I reach for fresh herbs in the summertime or dried ones in the winter and a bit of butter, then slip them under the breast skin before baking. When there's absolutely no time, I just put the chicken in the oven. Be sure to place the chicken on a rack above a shallow roasting pan for perfect air circulation. To turn this into a one-dish meal, add some vegetables—carrot chunks, potato cubes, onion wedges, fennel sticks, cut-up zucchini, or anything in season. Roast them in a single layer in a shallow baking pan beneath the chicken. Following this basic recipe, I give my favorite variations. ■ Makes 4 to 6 servings

Whole Roast Chicken

One 3^1/$_2$-pound whole broiler-fryer chicken

2 tablespoons butter, cut up

2 teaspoons kosher salt

1 teaspoon coarsely ground black pepper

1. Position the oven racks so that the top rack is in the center of the oven to allow room for the chicken. Place the other rack or racks below. Preheat the oven to convection roast at 450°F. Coat a rack with nonstick spray and set it on a shallow roasting pan.

2. Rinse the chicken and pat dry with paper towels. Loosen the skin over the breast and slide a 1^1/$_2$-teaspoon piece of butter under each side. Rub the remaining tablespoon of butter over the surface of the chicken and sprinkle with the salt and pepper. Place the chicken, breast side up, on the baking rack and tuck the wings under the shoulders (see Note).

3. Place the chicken in its pan in the oven and roast it for 35 minutes, then reduce the temperature to 300°F and roast for 25 to 30 more minutes or until the juices run clear and an instant-read thermometer inserted into the inside of the thigh meat reads 170°F.

4. Transfer the chicken to a warm platter, cover loosely with foil, and let it rest for about 15 minutes before carving.

Note: For aesthetic reasons, many cooks like to truss the bird, that is, tie the legs together. This inhibits the heat from reaching the inner thigh meat, which increases the roasting time. During this time the breast meat can become very dry and overcooked. I prefer not to truss the bird at all, especially if I have planned to carve it in the kitchen.

Herb Roasted Whole Chicken

Mix ^{1}/$_2$ teaspoon each of dried basil, dried lavender, dried marjoram, dried rosemary, dried sage, dried summer savory, dried thyme, and fennel seeds in a coffee or spice grinder and grind until powdered. (You can use 4 teaspoons herbes de Provence in place of this mixture.) Rub the chicken inside and outside with olive oil and pat the herb mixture on evenly all over. Place the chicken on the roasting rack and roast as directed. Remove to a carving board and serve.

Asian-Spiced Roast Whole Chicken

Mix 2 tablespoons vegetable oil, 1 tablespoon minced garlic, and 1^1/$_2$ teaspoons five-spice powder. Rub the mixture over the chicken and roast as directed. After roasting, serve the chicken on a platter surrounded with fresh cilantro.

Curry Roasted Chicken with Lime Juice

In a small pan, melt 4 tablespoons butter and add 1 tablespoon curry powder and 1 minced garlic clove. Sprinkle the chicken with kosher salt and freshly ground black pepper and brush with the curry butter. Roast as directed, brushing the chicken with the curry butter several times. Transfer the roasted chicken to a carving board, cover loosely with foil, and let it rest for about 15 minutes before carving. Meanwhile, pour off the fat from the roasting pan and set the pan over moderate heat. Add $^1/_2$ cup water and bring to a boil. Scrape the pan to loosen the browned bits, bring the liquid to a boil, and reduce it to 3 tablespoons. Add any juices that have accumulated from the roasted chicken, 1 teaspoon freshly squeezed lime juice, and kosher salt and freshly ground black pepper to taste. Serve the juices with the chicken.

Marinated Whole Chicken with Garlic and Rosemary

The day before you plan to cook the chicken, wash it, dry it, and place it into a large zip-top plastic bag. Add $^1/_4$ cup freshly squeezed lemon juice, $^1/_2$ cup dry white wine, 1 teaspoon dried rosemary, 4 peeled and coarsely chopped garlic cloves, and $^1/_4$ cup olive oil. Seal the bag and refrigerate overnight, turning the bag once or twice. The next day, preheat the oven, remove the chicken from the bag, place it on the roasting rack, and roast as directed, brushing the chicken every 15 minutes with the marinade. Transfer the chicken to a carving board and serve.

Roast Chicken with Fennel Seeds

Combine 2 minced garlic cloves, 3 tablespoons fennel seeds, 1 teaspoon kosher salt, and $^1/_2$ teaspoon freshly ground black pepper. Loosen the skin on the breast of the chicken and spread the garlic mixture evenly over the breast, back, and legs. Roast as directed, brushing with olive oil once or twice. Transfer the roasted chicken to a carving board and serve.

This is a simple country-style roast chicken with a garlicky wine marinade. Roast small red or fingerling potatoes while the chicken cooks. Add them to the oven after the chicken has cooked for 15 minutes. You can even add a pan of popovers (page 191) to the oven. They will be done in about 1 hour. ■ Makes 3 to 4 servings

Wine-Marinated Chicken

One 3- to 4-pound whole roasting chicken
3/4 cup dry white wine
1 tablespoon dried oregano
4 garlic cloves, coarsely chopped
1/4 cup olive oil, plus more for potatoes
12 small red or fingerling potatoes, optional
Kosher salt

1. Rinse the chicken and pat dry with paper towels; place it into a zip-top plastic bag. Add the wine, oregano, garlic, and 1/4 cup olive oil and close the bag. Refrigerate overnight, turning the bag once or twice.

2. Position the oven racks so that the top rack is in the center of the oven. Preheat the oven to convection roast at 325°F. Coat a rack with nonstick spray for the chicken and set it on a shallow roasting pan.

3. To prepare the potatoes, if using, scrub small red or fingerling potatoes, pat dry, and toss them with olive oil to coat lightly; sprinkle them with salt. Put them in a shallow baking pan or on a rimmed cookie sheet, place it on a rack beneath the chicken, and roast them for 45 minutes, until tender.

4. Remove the chicken from the bag and place on the rack over the shallow roasting pan. Tie the legs together and roast for 55 minutes to an hour, until the chicken is golden and an instant-read thermometer inserted into the center of the thigh reads 170° to 175°F. Remove the chicken from the rack, let it rest for 15 minutes, and carve on a board.

I've discovered that poultry really *is* juicier and more flavorful when it is brined. But the amazing thing is that when you add spices to the brine, the chicken picks up the flavors. I threw in a couple tablespoons of a special hot chimayo chile powder bought on a whim. Not only did the rich chile flavor come through, but the chicken also had just a pleasant hint of hotness. Convection roasting adds another measure of juiciness to the chicken, sealing in the juices. Sometimes I scrub a couple of baking potatoes, rub them with olive oil, and place them in the oven to roast right along with the chicken. ■ Makes 4 to 6 servings

Roasted Chile-Brined Chicken

One 3^1/2- to 4-pound whole broiler-fryer
1 cup kosher salt
^{1}/2 cup packed brown sugar
2 tablespoons chimayo chile powder or regular
   chili powder

1. Rinse the chicken. Combine 5 quarts water, the salt, sugar, and chile powder in a large pail or storage container. Place the chicken in the container, cover, and refrigerate for 24 hours.

2. Position the oven racks so that the top rack is in the center of the oven. Preheat the oven to convection roast at 325°F. Remove the chicken from the brine and dry it well with paper towels.

3. Coat the roasting rack with nonstick spray and place the chicken on the rack over a shallow roasting pan. Place into the oven and roast for 60 to 70 minutes or until the juices run clear or an instant-read thermometer inserted into the inner part of the thigh reads 170° to 175°F.

4. Remove the chicken from the oven, cover with foil, and let rest for 10 minutes before carving.

Maple-Brined Chicken
Substitute 1 cup pure maple syrup for the brown sugar.

Crunchy with peanuts and marinated in a richly flavored Asian-style sauce, this is good with steamed jasmine rice and stir-fried snow peas. ■ Makes 4 to 6 servings

Chutney-Hoisin Chicken Thighs

4 large garlic cloves, minced

2 to 3 quarter-sized fresh ginger slices, peeled and finely chopped

$^1/_2$ cup hoisin sauce

$^1/_4$ cup mango chutney

2 tablespoons rice wine vinegar

$^3/_4$ teaspoon freshly ground black pepper

2 tablespoons sesame oil

8 to 12 chicken thighs, skinned and trimmed

$^1/_3$ cup finely chopped peanuts, salted and dry-roasted

Corn oil

1. Position the oven racks so that they are evenly spaced and one rack is in the center of the oven. Preheat the oven to convection roast at 425°F.

Cover a shallow baking pan or broiler pan with foil and coat with nonstick spray.

2. In a large bowl, mix together the garlic, ginger, hoisin sauce, chutney, vinegar, pepper, and sesame oil.

3. Rinse the chicken thighs and pat dry with paper towels and coat with the sauce. Roll in the chopped peanuts. Place the chicken on the prepared pan and drizzle with corn oil.

4. Place the pan on the center rack and roast for 25 to 30 minutes or until the thighs are no longer pink in the center, juices run clear, and instant thermometer reads 170°F.

Roast Chicken Quarters

Two 3-pound chickens, quartered

1 teaspoon kosher salt

$^1/_2$ teaspoon freshly ground black pepper

7 tablespoons butter, cut into pieces

1. Position the oven racks so that they are evenly spaced and one rack is in the center of the oven. Preheat the oven to convection roast at 425°F. Cover a shallow baking pan or broiler pan with foil and coat with nonstick spray.

2. Rinse the chicken and pat dry with paper towels. Sprinkle with the salt and pepper and dot with the butter. Place in the center of the oven and roast for 25 to 30 minutes, basting with the pan juices twice, until the juices run clear.

3. While the chicken roasts, prepare one of the following sauces, if desired.

Roast Chicken Quarters in Old-Fashioned Country Milk Gravy

Transfer the chicken to a warm serving dish. Skim excess fat from the pan drippings, then pour the defatted juices into a skillet. Heat to boiling. With a whisk, stir in $^1/_4$ cup all-purpose flour and cook over medium heat for about 2 minutes. Whisk in 1 cup warmed whole milk and continue cooking and stirring until the gravy is smooth. Add kosher salt and freshly ground black pepper to taste. Pour the sauce over the chicken.

Roast Chicken Quarters in Chinese Herb Sauce

Transfer the chicken to a warm serving dish. Skim excess fat from the pan drippings, then pour the defatted juices into a skillet. Add 2 tablespoons sesame oil, 4 minced garlic cloves, 1 tablespoon peeled and grated fresh ginger, and 1 bunch trimmed and sliced green onions. In a medium bowl, combine 1 cup chicken broth, $^1/_4$ cup dry sherry, $^1/_4$ cup hoisin sauce, 1 tablespoon soy sauce, 1 teaspoon sugar, $^1/_2$ teaspoon hot Chinese chili sauce, and 2 tablespoons cornstarch. Cook, stirring, until the sauce thickens. Adjust the seasonings to taste. Pour the sauce over the chicken and sprinkle with $1/4$ cup chopped fresh cilantro. Serve with steamed rice.

Butter and Rosemary Roast Chicken

Rub the chicken quarters with 4 tablespoons melted butter and season with 2 tablespoons chopped fresh rosemary and 1 teaspoon kosher salt. Roast as directed above.

Lemon Chicken

Sprinkle the chicken quarters with kosher salt and freshly ground black pepper. Place on a roasting pan and surround with 1 pound baking potatoes, peeled and thickly sliced. Sprinkle the potatoes with 3 chopped garlic cloves and 2 tablespoons chopped fresh oregano, or 1 teaspoon dried. Pour 1 cup freshly squeezed lemon juice over the chicken and bake for 25 to 30 minutes, until the potatoes are tender and the chicken juices run clear.

While the chicken roasts (it only takes about 30 minutes), prepare one of these sauces to dress it up, or simply serve with mashed potatoes and gravy prepared with the pan drippings.

■ Makes 8 servings

Crusty Chicken Breasts with Cilantro Tomato Sauce

4 skinless, boneless chicken breast halves

1 tablespoon freshly squeezed lime juice

1 tablespoon honey

$2/3$ cup crushed corn tortilla chips

One $14^1/2$-ounce can diced tomatoes

$1/4$ cup chopped fresh cilantro

1 garlic clove, minced

$1/2$ teaspoon dried oregano, preferably Mexican

$1/2$ cup shredded Monterey Jack

Fresh cilantro sprigs and lime wedges for garnish

Cooked rice

My husband loves tortilla chips, but he won't touch those little pieces left in the bottom of the bag, so I crush them with a rolling pin to make a coating for boneless chicken breasts. This family favorite can be easily expanded into a party meal. Ordinarily, I serve this with rice, and sometimes I like to add black beans, too.

■ Makes 4 servings

1. Position the oven racks so that there is a rack in the center of the oven. Preheat the oven to convection bake at 475°F. Cover a shallow baking pan with foil and coat with nonstick spray.

2. Rinse the chicken breasts and dry with paper towels. Mix together the lime juice and honey. Dip the chicken breasts in the mixture, then coat both sides in the tortilla chips. Place on the prepared baking pan.

3. Bake for 15 to 20 minutes, until the chicken breasts are cooked through and the coating is lightly browned.

4. Meanwhile, in a food processor fitted with the steel blade or a blender, process the tomatoes with their juice, the cilantro, garlic, and oregano until smooth. Pour the mixture into a 2-quart saucepan and boil until reduced to $1^1/4$ cups, 4 to 5 minutes.

5. Sprinkle the chicken with the cheese and return it to the oven just until the cheese melts, about 1 minute. Spoon the sauce onto dinner plates and place the chicken on top. Garnish with cilantro and lime wedges and serve with rice.

This simple sweet-hot glaze is one to remember when you're down to the wire at dinnertime. Keep the ingredients on hand in your cupboard, ready to dress up ordinary chicken parts. Cover leftover glaze and store it in the refrigerator; it will keep for several weeks. In the convection oven, the chicken cooks quickly, retaining its tenderness and juiciness. ■ Makes 6 servings

Hot Pepper Chicken

$^1/_3$ cup hot pepper jelly
$^1/_3$ cup Dijon mustard
$^1/_3$ cup honey
6 skinless, boneless chicken breast halves
1 to 2 tablespoons pine nuts for garnish
Steamed rice

1. Position the oven racks so that there is a rack in the center of the oven. Preheat the oven to convection bake at 400°F. Cover a shallow baking pan with foil and coat with nonstick spray.

2. Combine the jelly, mustard, and honey. Rinse and dry the chicken breasts. Arrange the chicken breasts in a shallow baking dish and spread them evenly with the mustard mixture. Bake for 15 to 20 minutes or until the chicken is cooked through. Sprinkle with pine nuts during the last minute of cooking. Remove the chicken from the oven and serve with rice.

Moroccan Spiced Chicken Breasts

6 skinless, boneless chicken breast halves

1 small onion

$^1/_2$ cup chopped fresh flat-leaf parsley

$^1/_2$ cup chopped fresh cilantro

$^1/_2$ cup freshly squeezed lemon juice

$^1/_4$ cup olive oil

1 teaspoon kosher salt

2 teaspoons grated fresh ginger

2 garlic cloves

$^1/_2$ teaspoon ground cumin

$^1/_2$ teaspoon sweet paprika

$^1/_2$ teaspoon ground ginger

$^1/_2$ teaspoon freshly ground black pepper

Steamed couscous

1. Rinse the chicken breasts and pat dry with paper towels. Place in a glass or nonreactive dish.

2. Combine the remaining ingredients, except the couscous, in a food processor fitted with the steel blade or a blender and process until pureed. Pour the mixture over the chicken breasts, cover, and refrigerate for 2 hours or overnight.

3. Position the oven racks so that the top rack is 6 inches from the top of the oven. Preheat the oven to convection roast at 400°F. Cover a shallow-rimmed baking pan with foil and coat with nonstick spray.

4. Remove the chicken breasts from the marinade and place on the baking pan. Place the pan on the top rack and roast for 15 to 20 minutes, until cooked through. Do not overcook. Serve the chicken with seasoned, steamed couscous, prepared according to package directions.

I've baked these spicy chicken breasts for crowds, and always receive lots of compliments. The original recipe was for grill-cooking, but this version works year-round. ■ Makes 6 servings

> You can double or triple this recipe, although you probably won't need to increase the egg mixture until the recipe is quadrupled. ■ Makes 4 servings

Oven-Fried Chicken with Potato Wedges and Green Sauce

4 skinless, boneless chicken breast halves

1 egg

2 tablespoons milk

1 cup crushed plain cornflakes

1 teaspoon celery salt

4 medium to large potatoes, scrubbed and each
   cut lengthwise into 4 wedges

3 tablespoons olive oil

2 cups fresh parsley leaves, preferably flat-leaf

2 green onions, trimmed and sliced crosswise,
   including some of the green tops

2 tablespoons drained capers

2 teaspoons white balsamic vinegar

Kosher salt and freshly ground black pepper

1. Position the oven racks so that there is a rack in the center of the oven. Preheat the oven to convection bake at 475°F. Cover a baking sheet with foil and coat with nonstick spray.

2. Rinse the chicken breasts and pat dry with paper towels.

3. Mix the egg and milk and place in a shallow pan. Combine the cornflakes and celery salt in another shallow pan or plate. Dip the chicken pieces first in the egg-milk mixture, then roll them in the cornflakes mixture. Place on the prepared baking sheet.

4. Coat the potato wedges with 1 tablespoon of the olive oil. Arrange skin side down around the chicken breasts on the baking sheet. Roast them in the center of the oven for 15 to 20 minutes or until the potatoes are tender and lightly browned, and the chicken breasts are cooked.

5. Combine the parsley, green onions, capers, vinegar, and remaining 2 tablespoons olive oil in a blender or a food processor fitted with the steel blade. Process until pureed. Add salt and pepper to taste.

6. Serve each chicken breast with a spoonful of the sauce, surrounded by 4 potato wedges.

Roast a selection of seasonal vegetables right along with the chicken breasts to make a delicious meal. Turnips, carrots, onions, and potatoes are perfect for a winter evening.

■ Makes 4 servings

Parmesan-Rosemary Chicken Breasts with Root Vegetables

4 skinless, boneless chicken breast halves

$3/4$ cup plain dried bread crumbs, purchased or homemade (see Note)

$1/3$ cup freshly grated Parmesan

2 teaspoons dried rosemary

$1/2$ teaspoon kosher salt

$1/4$ teaspoon freshly ground black pepper

4 tablespoons ($1/2$ stick) butter, melted

FOR THE ROOT VEGETABLES

2 turnips, peeled and cut into $1/2$-inch cubes

2 red potatoes, scrubbed and cut into 1-inch cubes

2 medium carrots, peeled and cut into $1/2$-inch diagonal slices

2 red onions, peeled and each cut lengthwise into 4 wedges

1 tablespoon melted butter or vegetable or olive oil

$1/2$ teaspoon kosher salt

1. Position the oven racks so that there is a rack in the center of the oven. Preheat the oven to convection roast at 475°F. Cover a shallow-rimmed baking pan or roasting pan with foil and coat with nonstick spray.

2. Rinse the chicken breasts and pat dry with paper towels. In a shallow pan combine the bread crumbs, Parmesan, rosemary, salt, and pepper. Put the melted butter into another pan.

3. Roll the chicken breasts first in the melted butter, then in the crumb mixture. Place the chicken well apart on the prepared baking pan.

4. To make the root vegetables, toss the prepared vegetables in the butter and the salt. Scatter the vegetables in the pan around the chicken.

5. Roast the chicken in the center of the oven for 15 to 20 minutes, until the vegetables are tender and the chicken breasts are cooked through. Remove from the oven and serve.

Note: To make bread crumbs, put dry white bread in a food processor fitted with the steel blade or a blender and pulverize it.

Fragrant with garlic, lemon juice, and butter, this may just become a favorite. Soak up the tasty pan juices with crusty French bread. ■ Makes 4 servings

Roasted Chicken Breasts in Garlic Butter

4 skinless, boneless chicken breast halves

4 large garlic cloves, minced

$1/4$ cup freshly squeezed lemon juice

8 tablespoons (1 stick) butter, melted

1 teaspoon dried oregano

1 teaspoon kosher salt

$3/4$ teaspoon freshly ground black pepper

Pinch cayenne pepper

1 loaf French bread, cut into thick slices

1. Position the oven racks so that there is a rack in the center of the oven. Preheat the oven to convection roast at 475°F. Cover a shallow baking pan with foil.

2. Rinse the chicken breasts and pat dry with paper towels. In a small bowl, mix together the garlic, lemon juice, butter, oregano, salt, black pepper, and cayenne and pour into the baking pan.

3. Place the chicken breasts in the garlic-butter sauce and turn them to coat all sides, leaving the cut sides down to absorb more flavor.

4. Roast the chicken in the center of the oven for 20 minutes, until the chicken breasts are no longer pink in the center. Place on serving plates and spoon the hot sauce over each. Serve with the French bread.

Roast turkey is synonymous with autumn holiday celebrations. Because of the dangers of bacterial contamination, I prefer to bake bread-based turkey stuffing separately and stuff the turkey with garlic and herbs. Recipes for a variety of tasty glazes follow below. Check the guidelines chart for roasting time and temperature depending on the size of the turkey you are cooking. With turkeys up to 14 pounds, you can bake two or three accompaniment dishes— I suggest Creamy Garlic Potatoes (page 144) or Sweet Potatoes or Yams Roasted with Orange (page 145)—on the very bottom rack of the oven.

■ Makes about 1 serving per pound

Roast Whole Turkey with Garlic and Herb Stuffing

1 fresh turkey, 8 to 24 pounds

Kosher salt and freshly ground black pepper

6 to 12 whole garlic cloves, peeled

1 to 2 large sweet onions, peeled and quartered

1 bunch fresh sage

1 bunch fresh thyme

1 bunch fresh flat-leaf parsley

2 tablespoons butter, softened

Glaze of your choice (recipes follow)

Creamy Garlic Potatoes (page 144) or Sweet
    Potatoes or Yams Roasted with Orange (page
    145), optional

1. Remove the turkey from the refrigerator and let it stand at room temperature for an hour before roasting.

2. Position the oven racks so that the top rack is below the center of the oven and there is one rack of space beneath it (you may need to remove one oven rack), and place the bottom rack in the lowest position possible to accommodate accompaniment dishes on that rack. If the turkey is too large, you may need to use the whole oven for it and bake accompaniment dishes separately. Preheat the oven to convec-

tion roast at 325°F for turkeys 8 to 14 pounds. Preheat the oven to convection roast at 300°F for turkeys up to 24 pounds.

3. Rinse the turkey inside and out and pat dry with paper towels. Trim off and discard excess fat. Season the turkey inside with salt and pepper. Place the garlic, onions, and herbs inside the cavity of the turkey. Truss the turkey, if desired, using kitchen twine and tuck the wings behind the shoulders. Spread the butter over the turkey breast and season the turkey surface with additional salt and pepper.

4. Place the turkey, breast side up, on a rack in a shallow roasting pan. Insert a meat thermometer or probe into the thigh, away from the bone. Roast according to the following *estimated* times or until the probe or meat thermometer registers 170°F to 175°F:

8-pound turkey   1 to $1^1/4$ hours at 325°F
12-pound turkey $1^3/4$ to $2^1/4$ hours at 325°F
14-pound turkey $2^1/4$ to 3 hours at 325°F
18-pound turkey   3 to $3^1/2$ hours at 300°F
20-pound turkey $3^1/2$ to $3^3/4$ hours at 300°F
24-pound turkey $3^3/4$ to $4^1/4$ hours at 300°F

(continued)

5. Prepare one of the glazes below, and brush the turkey with it several times during the last 15 to 30 minutes. Prepare the potato dishes, if desired, and place on the bottom rack of the oven to cook along with the turkey. At this low temperature, the potatoes and the turkey will take about the same amount of time. If you cook potatoes at the same time, remove them when done and keep warm.

6. When the turkey is done, transfer it to a warmed platter, cover loosely with foil, and let rest for 20 to 30 minutes before carving.

Orange Honey Glaze

Combine $3/4$ cup orange marmalade, $3/4$ cup freshly squeezed orange juice, and 1 tablespoon honey in a small saucepan. Bring to a boil and boil for 1 minute. Brush the turkey with this mixture during the last 15 minutes of roasting.

Apricot Jalapeño Glaze

Combine $2/3$ cup apricot preserves, 3 seeded and chopped jalapeños, 2 tablespoons butter, and 1 tablespoon freshly squeezed lime juice in a small saucepan and bring to a boil; simmer for 5 minutes. Brush the turkey with this mixture during the last 15 minutes of roasting.

Maple Balsamic Glaze

Combine $1/2$ cup pure maple syrup, 2 tablespoons butter, and 2 tablespoons balsamic vinegar in a small saucepan and heat, stirring, until the butter is melted. Brush the turkey with this mixture during the last 15 minutes of roasting.

Bourbon and Mustard Glaze

Combine $3/4$ cup bourbon, $1/4$ cup spicy brown mustard, and 1 tablespoon brown sugar. Brush the turkey with this mixture during the last 15 minutes of roasting.

Cornish Hens with Wild Rice–Cranberry Stuffing and Jalapeño Jelly Glaze

FOR THE GLAZE

$1/2$ cup jalapeño jelly, or $1/2$ cup apple jelly with
   $1/2$ teaspoon Tabasco sauce
$1/4$ cup freshly squeezed orange juice
1 tablespoon balsamic vinegar
2 teaspoons Dijon mustard

Six 12-ounce Cornish game hens

FOR THE STUFFING

2 tablespoons butter
$1/2$ cup finely chopped onion
$1/2$ cup chicken broth
$1/2$ cup dried cranberries
$1/4$ cup chopped, toasted hazelnuts or filberts
1 tablespoon freshly grated orange zest
2 teaspoons dried poultry seasoning
$1/2$ teaspoon kosher salt
3 cups cooked wild rice

Butter for basting hens

This simple recipe might well replace a turkey for a special holiday meal. The even browning that the convection oven offers and repeated basting with the slightly spicy glaze guarantee beautifully burnished, succulent little birds.

■ Makes 6 servings (1 hen per person)

1. Position the oven racks so that there is a rack in the center of the oven. Preheat the oven to convection roast at 350°F. Coat a shallow roasting pan or broiler pan and rack with non-stick spray.

(continued)

2. To make the glaze, in a small saucepan, heat the jalapeño jelly until melted. Remove from the heat and stir in the orange juice, balsamic vinegar, and mustard. Set aside.

3. Rinse the hens and pat dry with paper towels. Set aside.

4. To make the stuffing, in a medium skillet, melt the butter and add the onion; sauté over medium-high heat for 5 minutes, stirring constantly, until the onion is translucent. Remove from the heat and stir in the chicken broth, cranberries, hazelnuts, orange zest, poultry seasoning, and salt. Stir in the cooked wild rice.

5. Stuff each hen with $^3/4$ cup of the wild rice mixture. Tie the legs together with the tail of each bird to close the opening. Place on the roasting pan. Brush with the glaze and roast for 20 minutes. Brush again with butter, then with the glaze, and roast in the center of the oven for 10 minutes at a time, until an instant-read thermometer inserted into the meaty portion of the thigh registers 175°F. This should take 25 to 30 more minutes. Baste the hens with any remaining glaze and keep warm until serving.

Butterflied game hens—split down the backbone and flattened, with the backbone removed—can be cooked at a higher temperature and in less time in the convection oven. You'll notice that the temperature is higher than with whole hens, because these hens are butterflied.

■ Makes 6 servings

Butterflied Deviled Game Hens

$^1/_2$ cup hot mustard (German, English, or Chinese)

1 large shallot

3 tablespoons cider vinegar

2 teaspoons honey

$^1/_2$ teaspoon freshly ground black pepper

Three 16- to 20-ounce Cornish game hens, backbone removed and butterflied

4 tablespoons ($^1/_2$ stick) melted butter

1. Position the oven racks so that the top rack is 6 to 8 inches from the top of the oven. Preheat the oven to convection roast at 425°F. Coat a shallow roasting pan or broiler pan and rack with nonstick spray.

2. Combine the mustard, shallot, vinegar, honey, and pepper in a food processor fitted with the steel blade or a blender and mix until smooth. Reserve $^1/_4$ cup of the mixture. Transfer the remaining mixture to a small bowl.   *(continued)*

3. Loosen the skin from the flesh of the hens' thighs and drumsticks with your fingers, being careful not to puncture the skin. Spread one-half of the mustard mixture smoothly between meat and skin. Place the hens on the prepared pan.

4. Roast for 10 minutes. Turn the hens over and baste with the butter and with the remaining mustard mixture. Roast for another 20 minutes. Turn again and baste with the butter and with the mustard mixture. Roast for 10 more minutes. Watch carefully; if the hens brown too much,

turn them again and brush them again with the butter and with the mustard mixture. Insert an instant-read thermometer into the thickest part of the thigh. The hens are done when the thermometer reads 175°F.

5. When the hens are done, baste them once more with the reserved mustard mixture to glaze. Serve with Pesto-Roasted Potatoes (page 141) or a Roasted Red Potato Salad (page 151).

Turkey Meat Loaf with Roasted Red Pepper and Tomato Sauce

1¹/2 cups finely chopped onion

3 garlic cloves, minced

1 teaspoon olive oil

1 medium carrot, cut into ¹/8-inch dice

³/4 pound portobello mushrooms, trimmed and
  finely chopped

1 teaspoon kosher salt

¹/2 teaspoon freshly ground black pepper

1 cup plain dried bread crumbs, purchased or
  homemade (see Note, page 106)

¹/3 cup milk

2 eggs

1¹/4 pounds ground turkey

2 tablespoons tomato chili sauce or ketchup

Roasted Red Pepper and Tomato Sauce (recipe
  follows)

1. Position the oven racks so that the top rack is in the center of the oven. Preheat the oven to convection roast at 375°F. Cover a baking sheet with foil and coat with nonstick spray.

2. In a large nonstick skillet over medium-high heat, cook the onion and garlic in the olive oil for about 2 minutes, until the onion is softened. Add the carrot and cook, stirring, for 3 more minutes; add the mushrooms, salt, and pepper. Cook until the mushroom liquid is evaporated and they are very tender, about 10 minutes. Transfer to a large bowl to cool.

3. Stir the bread crumbs, milk, and eggs together in a large bowl. Add the turkey, the tomato chili sauce, and the sautéed vegetables and mix until well blended. Shape into an oval loaf about 9 inches long and 3 inches high and place on the prepared baking sheet. Insert the oven probe and set to 170°F.

4. Roast in the center of the oven for 45 to 55 minutes or until the probe indicates that the meat loaf is done or an instant-read thermometer inserted into the center of the loaf registers 170°F.

5. Meanwhile, make the Roasted Red Pepper and Tomato Sauce, and serve it with slices of the meat loaf.   *(continued)*

Roast the tomatoes,
peppers, and garlic right
along with the meat loaf
to make the sauce.

■ Makes 6 servings

Roasted Red Pepper and Tomato Sauce

Not only is this sauce delicious with meat loaf, it also goes well with roasted chicken or salmon. ■ Makes about 1 cup

1 garlic head

4 medium plum (Roma) tomatoes, halved
    lengthwise (about $1/2$ pound)

Kosher salt

1 large red bell pepper, stemmed, seeded, and
    quartered

1 teaspoon olive oil

$1^1/2$ teaspoons freshly squeezed lemon juice

$1/2$ teaspoon balsamic vinegar

1. Preheat the oven to convection roast at 375°F. Cover a baking sheet with foil and coat with nonstick spray.

2. Cut off and discard the top quarter of the garlic head and wrap the head in foil. Arrange the tomatoes, cut sides up, on the baking sheet; sprinkle with salt. Add the pepper, skin side up, and the garlic head to the pan. Roast the vegetables in the center or top third of the oven for 45 to 55 minutes, until soft. Remove the pepper after 20 minutes and wrap it in foil. When the pepper is cooled, remove and discard the skin.

3. Put the pepper and tomatoes into a food processor fitted with the steel blade or a blender. Squeeze the roasted garlic cloves out of their skins and add to the tomatoes and peppers along with the olive oil, lemon juice, and vinegar. Puree the sauce until smooth.

Note: If making this sauce to serve with Turkey Meat Loaf, cook it at the same time, on a rack beneath the meat loaf.

Fish and Shellfish

There is nothing to compare with fresh fish, simply prepared. The most splendid fish I ever ate was in Stavanger, Norway, at a little restaurant on a pier. The menu listed at least two hundred varieties of fish, and when you put in your order, a runner from the kitchen bought it from the fish market some fifty feet away. It doesn't come fresher than that. Since the pleasure of having fish fresh from the water is only for those who live near the sea or a lake, the rest of us do the best we can with what we can find.

I have a friend who is a commercial fisherman in Alaska. Each summer he catches thousands of pounds of salmon and halibut. Frozen within minutes of the catch, and kept solidly frozen until it reaches its destination, the fish is as fresh as anything we could hope to find in any market.

Frozen fish needs to be kept at a constant temperature of zero degrees and when you get it, it should be solidly frozen. A block of juices at the bottom of a package is proof that the fish has been thawed and refrozen. Before cooking, thaw the fish in the refrigerator or under cold running water.

It takes a very hot oven to roast this fish, and the results are incredible! The halibut is gently browned on the outside. You'd never be able to accomplish this "blast of hot air" in a conventional oven because the circulating heat hits everything at one time. Sometimes I add a few baby potatoes, scrubbed and quartered, or a quartered fennel bulb, tossed in melted butter and scattered around the fish. They'll be done at the same time as the halibut. ■ Makes 4 servings

Halibut Roasted with Garlic-Parsley Butter

One 1¹/₂-pound halibut fillet, thawed if frozen
8 tablespoons (1 stick) melted butter
2 tablespoons minced fresh flat-leaf parsley
2 to 3 garlic cloves, minced
Kosher salt and freshly ground black pepper

1. Position the oven racks so that the top rack is 5 to 6 inches from the top of the oven. Preheat the oven to convection roast at 500°F. Cover a shallow-rimmed roasting pan with foil and coat with nonstick spray.

2. Rinse the fish and pat dry with paper towels. Center it on the pan. Mix the butter, parsley, and garlic together. Brush the fish on both sides with the mixture.

3. Roast the fish for 10 minutes, until it flakes when tested with a fork. Brush with any remaining butter mixture and sprinkle with salt and pepper. Transfer it to a warm serving platter.

Fish with a Lemon-Dill Crust

1 cup milk

One 1^1/2-pound halibut, cod, tilapia, or other lean, white fish fillet, ^{1}/2 to 1 inch thick, thawed if frozen

^{1}/2 cup mayonnaise

^{1}/4 cup chopped fresh dill

1 tablespoon Dijon mustard

2 teaspoons freshly grated lemon zest

^{1}/4 teaspoon kosher salt

^{1}/4 teaspoon freshly ground pepper, preferably white

^{3}/4 cup cornflakes, crushed

1. In a large zip-top plastic bag, combine the milk and fish; seal and let soak for 20 to 30 minutes.

2. Position the oven racks so that the top rack is 5 to 6 inches from the top of the oven. Preheat the oven to convection roast at 500°F. Cover a shallow-rimmed roasting pan with foil and coat with nonstick spray.

3. In a small bowl, combine the mayonnaise, dill, mustard, lemon zest, salt, and pepper and mix well.

4. Drain the fish, pat dry with paper towels, and discard the milk. Spread the mayonnaise mixture over the fish and top with the cornflakes. Place the fish on the prepared pan.

5. Place the pan on the top rack in the oven and roast for 12 to 15 minutes or until the fish flakes easily when tested with a fork.

A coating of herbed mayonnaise keeps the fish moist while it bakes.

■ Makes 4 servings

This is a fast and easy method for preparing firm, thick fish fillets. A heavy skillet with a ridged bottom will produce nice grill marks when preheated in the oven. Serve this fish with stir-fried Asian noodles or spaghetti tossed with sautéed bok choy, green onions, and any type of sprouts, seasoned with minced garlic, ginger, rice vinegar, and sesame oil. ■ Makes 4 servings

Oven-Grilled Halibut, Flounder, or Sea Bass

1 pound firm fish fillets, such as halibut, flounder, or sea bass (about 4 pieces)
2 tablespoons vegetable oil
1 teaspoon sesame oil
$^{1}/_{4}$ teaspoon hot chili oil
2 garlic cloves, minced
1 tablespoon freshly grated lemon zest
$^{1}/_{2}$ teaspoon kosher salt
$^{1}/_{8}$ teaspoon freshly ground pepper, preferably white

1. Position the oven racks so that the top rack is 5 to 6 inches from the top of the oven. Coat a ridged cast-iron skillet with nonstick spray and place it in the oven on the top rack. Preheat the oven to convection roast at 500°F.

2. Rub the fish fillets with the vegetable, sesame, and chili oils. Mix the garlic, lemon zest, salt, and pepper and rub both sides of the fillets with the mixture. Place the fish on the preheated skillet and cook until lightly browned, about 3 minutes.

3. Turn the fish over carefully and cook for 5 to 7 more minutes or until the fish flakes easily when tested with a fork but is still moist. Total cooking time is approximately 10 minutes.

Sesame-Citrus Tuna Steaks

$1/2$ cup soy sauce

$1/4$ cup honey

$1/4$ cup freshly squeezed orange juice

2 tablespoons sesame oil

2 garlic cloves, minced

1 slice fresh ginger, crushed (about $1/3$ inch thick)

1 teaspoon cornstarch

Four 6- to 8-ounce tuna steaks, 1 to $1^1/2$ inches thick

Olive oil

1. Combine the soy sauce, honey, orange juice, sesame oil, garlic, ginger, and cornstarch in a heavy, zip-top plastic bag and add the tuna steaks. Close the bag and marinate the fish for 2 to 4 hours in the refrigerator.

2. Position the oven racks so that the top rack is 6 inches from the top of the oven. Preheat the oven to convection roast at 500°F. Place a wire rack on top of a shallow-rimmed roasting pan. Rub the rack with oil.

3. Remove the tuna steaks from the marinade and rub with olive oil. Place on the rack in the roasting pan and roast for 5 to 6 minutes, turning once, until the surface of the tuna is browned but the center is still red.

Tuna steaks are delicious when the exterior is browned but the center is rare. These steaks can be done on an outdoor grill, but when that isn't feasible, the convection oven does a wonderful job.

■ Makes 4 servings

When I roast salmon steaks, I often like to start a pan of root vegetables in the oven 5 to 10 minutes before the salmon. I toss quartered potatoes and 1-inch chunks of parsnips and carrots with a small amount of olive oil. A complete meal is cooked in less than 20 minutes! ■ Makes 4 servings

Roasted Salmon Steaks with Tarragon Butter

4 salmon steaks, about 1 inch thick, about 2 to 2^1/$_2$ lbs
Olive oil
Kosher salt and freshly ground black pepper
FOR THE TARRAGON BUTTER
4 tablespoons (^{1}/$_2$ stick) butter, softened
1 tablespoon fresh tarragon, or 2 teaspoons dried
1 tablespoon red wine vinegar
Kosher salt and freshly ground black pepper

1. Position the oven racks so that the top rack is 6 inches from the top of the oven. Preheat the oven to convection roast at 500°F. Coat a shallow roasting pan and flat roasting rack with nonstick spray.

2. Rinse the salmon steaks under cold running water and pat dry with paper towels. Brush the steaks with olive oil on both sides and sprinkle lightly with salt and pepper.

3. Place the salmon on the roasting rack and roast on the top rack for 5 to 8 minutes or just until the fish flakes easily when tested with a fork.

4. To make the tarragon butter, cream the butter with the tarragon and red wine vinegar until blended and smooth. Add salt and pepper to taste. Serve about 1 tablespoonful of tarragon butter on each salmon steak.

Roasted Salmon Fillet with Onion Butter

1 whole salmon, filleted (4 to 5 pounds)

8 tablespoons (1 stick) butter

6 green onions, minced, including the green part

3 tablespoons soy sauce

1. Position the oven racks so that one rack is in the center of the oven. Preheat the oven to convection roast at 500°F. Cover a large, rimmed baking pan (a half sheet pan works well) with foil and coat with nonstick spray.

2. Pat the salmon fillets dry with paper towels and place on the prepared pan, skin side down.

3. In a skillet, heat the butter and add the green onions; sauté over medium heat until the onions are soft. Add the soy sauce.

4. Brush the salmon with the butter mixture. Roast it for 8 to 10 minutes or until the salmon is just cooked.

5. Remove the salmon from the oven and peel back the skin. Brush it with the remaining butter mixture. Transfer the salmon to a warmed serving platter to serve.

There's nothing quite so delicious as salmon roasted with soy-flavored butter as a final baste. In the convection oven it cooks amazingly fast. Remove from the oven just when the fish is done.

■ Makes 6 to 8 generous servings

Tandoori Chicken is a classic northern Indian dish. The word "tandoori" comes from the Hindi word "tandoor," a tall, cylindrical clay oven originally used in northern India to cook meat dishes and bread. Here, we use a tandoori spice mixture as a marinade for salmon. Traditionalists might balk, but when I'm in a hurry, I use a store-bought tandoori spice mixture. In the convection oven, the salmon cooks quickly and is moist and mildly fragrant. A minty cucumber-yogurt sauce adds an authentic flavor..

■ Makes 4 servings

Tandoori Salmon with Cucumber Sauce

3 pounds salmon fillets
1 cup plain yogurt
2 garlic cloves, minced
1 tablespoon peeled and grated fresh ginger
2^1/2 tablespoons Tandoori Seasoning (recipe follows)
1 tablespoon chopped fresh mint
Cucumber Yogurt Sauce (recipe follows)

1. Rinse the salmon and pat dry with paper towels. Cut it into 8 equal pieces. Place in a single layer on a rimmed plate or tray, skin side down.

2. Mix the yogurt with the garlic, ginger, and Tandoori Seasoning. Spread it evenly over the salmon pieces. Cover and refrigerate for 3 to 4 hours.

3. Arrange the oven racks so that the top rack is just above the center of the oven. Preheat the oven to convection roast at 500°F. Coat a rimmed baking sheet with nonstick spray and place the salmon on the pan. Roast for 8 to 10 minutes or just until the salmon is cooked.

4. Remove the salmon to a warmed serving tray, sprinkle with mint, and serve with the Cucumber Yogurt Sauce.

Tandoori Seasoning

Roasting brings out all the aromatics in this seasoning mix. ■ Makes about 1¹/4 cups

1/4 cup whole black peppercorns

1/4 cup whole coriander seeds

2 tablespoons black cardamom seeds

1/2 tablespoon cumin seeds

2 tablespoons paprika

2 tablespoons chili powder

2 tablespoons whole fenugreek

2 tablespoons whole cloves

1/4 teaspoon nutmeg

1. Position the oven racks so that they are evenly spaced. Preheat the oven to convection bake at 350°F. Combine the peppercorns, coriander seeds, cardamom seeds, and cumin seeds and spread in a shallow baking pan.

2. Place the pan on the center rack of the oven and roast for 20 minutes, until aromatic. Cool. Combine with the remaining spices in a coffee grinder or mortar and pestle and grind until finely pulverized.

3. Store in an airtight container.

Cucumber Yogurt Sauce

■ Makes 8 servings

1 cup plain yogurt

2 European-style cucumbers, peeled, seeded, and diced

1 garlic clove, minced

1 tablespoon chopped fresh mint

1¹/2 teaspoons chopped fresh flat-leaf parsley

1/2 teaspoon kosher salt

Combine all the ingredients and put in a serving bowl. Cover and refrigerate for at least an hour before serving.

This is a quick and easy main dish. Although most shrimp you buy have been frozen, this dish is absolutely superb made with fresh shrimp, the largest you can find. ■ Makes 4 servings

Shrimp with Garlic and Lemon on Pasta

4 ounces orecchiette or shell pasta

4 tablespoons ($^1/_2$ stick) butter

5 garlic cloves, minced

$^1/_4$ cup extra virgin olive oil

1 pound uncooked shrimp, peeled, deveined, rinsed, and dried

$^1/_2$ cup seasoned dried bread crumbs

Juice of 1 lemon (about 4 tablespoons)

2 fresh tomatoes, diced

$^1/_2$ pound Brussels sprouts or broccoli florets, cleaned and steamed until tender

Kosher salt and freshly ground black pepper to taste

$^1/_2$ cup freshly grated Parmesan

1. Position the oven racks so that the top rack is 6 to 8 inches from the top of the oven. Preheat the oven to convection roast at 500°F.

2. Bring a large pot of salted water to a boil; add the pasta and boil for 10 to 12 minutes, until al dente.

3. Meanwhile, melt the butter in a large skillet over medium heat. Add the garlic and olive oil. Cook for 1 minute, until the garlic is aromatic, but do not let it brown. Add the shrimp and toss to coat. Pour the shrimp (but not all the garlic mixture) into a shallow baking dish. Sprinkle with the bread crumbs and the lemon juice. Bake for 10 minutes, until the shrimp turn pink and the bread crumbs are browned.

4. Toss the pasta with the remaining olive oil and garlic mixture. Add the tomatoes and the hot, steamed Brussels sprouts. Add salt and pepper to taste. Top with the shrimp–bread crumb mixture and sprinkle with the Parmesan. Serve.

Roasted Shrimp and Mushrooms on Fresh Spinach

2 pounds uncooked shrimp, peeled, deveined,
    rinsed, and dried

1 large garlic clove, minced

$1^1/_2$ teaspoons kosher salt

1 teaspoon paprika

$^1/_2$ teaspoon cayenne pepper

Juice of 1 lemon

$^1/_4$ cup olive oil

$^1/_2$ pound whole baby mushrooms, cleaned

6 cups fresh baby spinach leaves

2 diced fresh tomatoes for garnish

1 cup crisp snow peas, strings removed and sliced
    diagonally into 1-inch pieces

1. Position the oven racks so that the top rack is 6 inches from the top of the oven. Preheat the oven to convection broil or convection roast at 500°F. Cover a large rimmed baking sheet with foil and coat with nonstick spray.

2. In a large bowl, combine the shrimp with the garlic, salt, paprika, cayenne, lemon juice, and olive oil. Add the mushrooms and toss until the shrimp and mushrooms are completely coated with the marinade. Pour it on the prepared baking sheet in a single layer.

3. Roast for 5 minutes; turn the shrimp and mushrooms over and roast for 2 more minutes.

4. Serve on a bed of fresh spinach leaves. Garnish with the tomatoes and snow peas.

Meals don't come much easier, quicker, or better than this!

■ Makes 6 servings

Vegetables

Convection roasting of vegetables is not only convenient to do, but it also makes for wonderful year-round eating because roasting concentrates the sugars in the vegetables. The effect is similar to grilling but with less hassle. Root vegetables like carrots, onions, rutabagas, parsnips, and sweet potatoes become especially sweet and succulent. Summer vegetables like eggplant, zucchini, tomatoes, asparagus, and green beans turn tender and fresh tasting. I roast my favorite ratatouille because it is so convenient.

When roasting a variety of vegetables, cook root vegetables such as carrots, parsnips, potatoes, and rutabagas together for the same length of time, as long as the pieces are similar in size. Cook softer vegetables such as bell peppers, onions, zucchini, eggplant, and mushrooms together because they take a little less time than root vegetables. I cook the cabbages together, because cauliflower, broccoli, and Brussels sprouts take about the same amount of time. Tender asparagus and green beans are best cooked separately so you can watch their progress.

Most vegetables can be roasted right along with meat or poultry on the rack beneath. However, if you are roasting the vegetables alone, place them in the center of the oven. If roasting more than one pan of vegetables, place one pan in the center of the oven and the other below it. Ovens have two, three, or four racks. You can roast on all four racks at the same time with good results using the times and temperatures given in the recipes.

Caramelized Roasted Onions

3 large onions, cut crosswise into $^1/_8$-inch slices
2 tablespoons olive oil
1$^1/_2$ teaspoons kosher salt
1 teaspoon sugar

1. Preheat the oven to convection bake at 400°F. Coat a shallow (1 inch deep) roasting pan or baking sheet with nonstick spray.

2. In a large bowl, toss the onions with the olive oil, salt, and sugar. Spread the onions in an even layer on the prepared pan. Roast for 15 to 20 minutes, stirring once or twice, until the onions are soft and lightly browned.

Caramelized onions, sweet and succulent, are so easy to prepare in the convection oven. They roast quickly and evenly to a golden caramel color. Serve them as a sandwich filling, a topping for croutons, or on top of grilled burgers. A mandoline makes easy work of slicing the onions.

■ Makes about 2 cups

Roasted Peppers

6 whole red bell peppers
2 teaspoons olive oil
Kosher salt

1. Position the oven racks so that the top rack is 5 inches from the top of the oven. Preheat the oven to convection roast at 500°F. Cover a rimmed baking sheet with foil and coat with nonstick spray.

2. Rinse the peppers and dry with paper towels, then coat them lightly with the olive oil and sprinkle with salt. Place the peppers well apart on the prepared baking sheet. Roast them on the top rack for 15 to 17 minutes, until the peppers are charred in spots.

3. Remove the peppers from the oven, wrap the foil in the pan around them as much as you can, and place them in a brown paper bag. Close the bag and let the peppers cool for at least 15 minutes.

4. Remove the skin and seeds from the peppers.

Roasted peppers are not only good by themselves but they're a tasty ingredient in spreads and appetizers. Here is my favorite roasting method.

Butter-Roasted Beets

1 bunch fresh beets (4 to 6)
Vegetable oil or olive oil
1 to 2 tablespoons butter

1. Preheat the oven to convection roast at 400°F.

2. Trim off the beet greens, leaving 2 inches of the stems on the beets. Scrub the beets well and dry with paper towels. Rub them with oil and place them on a shallow baking pan.

3. Roast for 30 minutes, until a toothpick inserted into the beets slides in easily. Remove from the oven and cool.

4. Slip off the skins and slice the beets into a shallow casserole. Top with dots of butter and reheat for 5 to 10 minutes before serving.

Both the beet greens and the root are favorite vegetables, making beets about the most edible of all vegetables. You can roast beets in the convection oven in less time than it takes to boil them, and you save a whole lot of mess, too! ■ Makes 4 to 6 servings

Maple-Roasted Winter Vegetables

6 red, yellow, or fingerling potatoes, scrubbed and cut into 6 wedges

6 medium carrots, peeled, halved lengthwise, and cut into 1-inch pieces

3 medium parsnips, peeled, quartered lengthwise, and cut into 1-inch pieces

2 garlic heads, separated into cloves and peeled

2 tablespoons pure maple syrup

1 tablespoon melted butter or olive oil

1 to 2 teaspoons kosher salt

Freshly ground black pepper

1. Position the oven racks so that they are evenly spaced. Preheat the oven to convection roast at 400°F. Cover a shallow-rimmed baking pan with foil and coat with nonstick spray.

2. Combine the potatoes, carrots, parsnips, and garlic and toss with the maple syrup, butter, salt, and pepper. Spread the vegetables in an even layer on the prepared pan.

3. Roast in the center of the oven for 25 to 30 minutes, until the vegetables are tender when pierced with a fork.

A pan of these vegetables cooks easily along with chicken, Cornish game hens, or pork roast. Consider adding a dessert to the oven, too. All three items can be baked on separate racks. Place the vegetables in the center and the dessert on the bottom rack.

■ Makes 4 to 6 servings

Roasted asparagus spears are crisp-tender with great flavor. They can be roasted at higher temperatures as well (400° to 500°F), in which case the roasting time is short (8 to 10 minutes). If you are roasting meat or poultry at 375°F, that temperature will be fine for the asparagus, too. Don't add the asparagus to the oven too soon or it will be overcooked ■ Makes 6 to 8 servings

Roasted Soy-and-Sesame Asparagus

1 1/2 pounds fresh asparagus, trimmed
1 tablespoon vegetable oil or melted butter
1 tablespoon sesame oil
1 tablespoon soy sauce

1. Position the oven racks so that they are evenly spaced. Preheat the oven to convection roast at 450°F. Cover a shallow baking or roasting pan with foil and coat with nonstick spray.

2. Toss the asparagus with the vegetable and sesame oils and the soy sauce. Arrange in a single layer on the prepared pan. (The asparagus can be prepared ahead, ready for roasting; it does not need to be refrigerated unless you prepare it a day ahead.)

3. Roast on the bottom rack (beneath a roast, if applicable) or on a rack in the center of the oven for 8 to 10 minutes, until the asparagus is crisp-tender.

Roasted Asparagus with Basil Pesto and Pine Nuts

Toss the asparagus with 2 tablespoons olive oil and sprinkle with 1/2 teaspoon kosher salt. Roast for 5 minutes. Sprinkle with 2 tablespoons pine nuts and finish roasting. Transfer the asparagus to a heated serving dish and coat with 2 to 3 tablespoons prepared basil pesto. Sprinkle with 1 tablespoon freshly grated Parmesan.

Roasted Baby Carrots with Fresh Thyme

1 pound baby carrots or regular carrots, peeled and
    cut in half lengthwise
1 tablespoon olive oil or vegetable oil
1 teaspoon fresh thyme
1 garlic clove, minced
Kosher salt and freshly ground black pepper

1. Position the oven racks so that they are evenly spaced. Preheat the oven to convection roast at 475°F. Cover a shallow baking pan with foil and coat with nonstick spray.

2. In a large bowl, mix the carrots with the olive oil, thyme, and garlic. Spread them in an even layer on the prepared pan.

3. Roast for 20 to 25 minutes, until the carrots are tender. Sprinkle with salt and pepper to taste.

When carrots are roasted, they develop a sweet flavor that thyme enhances. I serve these carrots with a beef pot roast and roasted potatoes. ■ Makes 4 servings

Honey enhances the natural sweetness in rutabagas and parsnips. This is a perfect side dish for a holiday menu.

■ Makes 6 servings

Honey-Lemon Rutabagas and Parsnips

2 medium rutabagas, peeled (about 2 pounds each)
4 large parsnips, peeled
6 tablespoons melted butter or olive oil
3 tablespoons honey
$1/2$ teaspoon ground allspice
Kosher salt and freshly ground black pepper
3 tablespoons freshly squeezed lemon juice

1. Position the racks so they are evenly spaced. Preheat the oven to convection roast at 425°F. Cover a shallow-rimmed baking pan or jelly roll pan with foil and coat with nonstick spray.

2. Cut the rutabagas and parsnips into $1/2$-inch sticks. Put them in a large bowl and toss with the butter, honey, allspice, salt, pepper, and lemon juice.

3. Spread the vegetables in an even layer on the prepared pan. Roast for 20 to 25 minutes or until tender and the edges are lightly browned.

This basic, versatile recipe can be adapted to just about any vegetable depending on what you have on hand. While the oven preheats, prepare the vegetables. Serve with oven-grilled chicken breasts and steamed rice. ■ Makes 4 servings

Stir-Fry Roasted Vegetables

1 tablespoon olive oil or vegetable oil
6 large garlic cloves, coarsely chopped
1 teaspoon oyster sauce
$^1\!/_2$ teaspoon sugar
1 pound assorted vegetables, such as asparagus, green beans, eggplant, mushrooms, and bell peppers, cut into 1-inch pieces
1 jalapeño, seeded and thinly sliced

1. Position the oven racks so that they are evenly spaced. Preheat the oven to convection roast at 450°F. Cover a heavy, rimmed baking pan with foil and coat with nonstick spray.

2. In a large bowl, toss the olive oil with the garlic, oyster sauce, sugar, vegetables, and jalapeño until all the vegetables are lightly coated with oil.

3. Spread the vegetables on the prepared pan and roast in the center or lower half of the oven for 10 minutes, until crisp-tender. Serve hot.

Ratatouille is a vegetable stew from the south of France, traditionally made by slow cooking. By roasting the vegetables in a hot convection oven, the juices, flavors, and colors are quickly sealed in and the vegetables are succulent and remain distinguishable. ■ Makes 6 to 8 servings

Roasted Ratatouille

One 1-pound large eggplant, trimmed and cut into
    1-inch cubes

4 garlic cloves, minced

2 large onions, cut into 1-inch cubes

4 medium zucchini, halved lengthwise and cut
    crosswise into 1-inch slices

1 red bell pepper, seeded and cut into 1-inch
    squares

2 tablespoons olive oil

3/4 teaspoon kosher salt

1/2 teaspoon freshly ground black pepper

3 large tomatoes, cut into 1-inch cubes

3 tablespoons chopped fresh basil

1/4 cup minced fresh flat-leaf parsley

1. Position the oven racks so that they are evenly spaced. Preheat the oven to convection roast at 475°F. Line a large rimmed cookie sheet with foil and coat with nonstick spray.

2. In a large mixing bowl, toss the eggplant, garlic, onions, zucchini, and bell pepper with the olive oil until the vegetables are coated with the oil. Sprinkle with salt and pepper. Spread the vegetables in an even layer on the prepared pan.

3. Place the pan of vegetables on the rack beneath the meat (if you are cooking a meat dish at the same time) or in the center of the oven and roast for 15 to 20 minutes, until tender and aromatic. Put the vegetables in a serving dish and add the tomatoes, basil, and parsley. Serve hot or at room temperature.

This is a wonderful Greek-style one-dish meal or a side dish for a party. Roasting brings out the flavors of the vegetables. You can prepare all the vegetables except the potatoes ahead of time. ■ Makes 8 servings

Herbed Roasted Vegetables with Feta and Olives

1 1/2 pounds tiny red or fingerling potatoes, halved or chunked

1 large red onion, cut into 1-inch pieces

2 garlic heads, separated into cloves and peeled

2 fennel bulbs, trimmed and cut into 8 wedges

2 red bell peppers, seeded and cut into 1 1/2-inch squares

1 eggplant, trimmed and cut into 1 1/2-inch pieces

3/4 pound baby carrots

1/2 pound green beans, cut into 2-inch lengths

1/2 cup olive oil

2 teaspoons kosher salt

1/2 teaspoon freshly ground black pepper

1/4 cup chopped fresh herbs, such as Greek oregano, marjoram, thyme, and rosemary

1/4 pound feta, crumbled

1 cup pitted Greek olives

Chopped fresh basil or flat-leaf parsley for garnish

1. Position the oven racks so that they are evenly spaced. Preheat the oven to convection bake at 475°F. Cover two rimmed baking sheets with foil and coat with nonstick spray.

2. If preparing the vegetables ahead of time, put the potatoes in water to cover with 1 tablespoon lemon juice. Combine all the remaining vegetables in a large bowl with the olive oil, salt, pepper, and herbs. (Drain the potatoes well and add to the vegetables at this point if they are prepared more than an hour in advance.)

3. Divide the vegetables between the prepared pans. Spread the vegetables in an even layer.

4. Roast on the center or lower oven rack for 15 to 20 minutes, stirring once, or until the vegetables are browned on the edges and can be pierced easily with a fork. Sprinkle with the feta and roast for 5 more minutes or just until the feta is soft. Remove from the oven and top with the olives and chopped basil.

Acorn Squash Stuffed with Roasted Root Vegetables

2 acorn squash, halved lengthwise and seeded

Kosher salt and freshly ground black pepper

2 medium turnips, peeled and cut into 1-inch pieces

3 medium parsnips, peeled and cut into 1-inch pieces

2 medium carrots, peeled and cut into 1-inch pieces

1 medium onion, peeled and cut into 1-inch pieces

2 tablespoons olive oil or vegetable oil

$^1/_2$ cup freshly squeezed orange or apple juice

2 tablespoons soy sauce

1 tablespoon dry sherry

1. Position the oven racks so that they are evenly spaced, with one rack in the center of the oven, the other above it, and a third rack, if you have one, below it. Preheat the oven to convection bake at 400°F. Cover two shallow baking pans, such as jelly roll pans, with foil and coat with nonstick spray or a light coating of butter.

2. Sprinkle the squash with salt and pepper and place them cut side down on one of the prepared pans.

3. In a large bowl, toss the turnips, parsnips, carrots, and onion with the olive oil until the vegetables are evenly coated. Spread the vegetables in an even layer on the second prepared pan.

4. Place the squash on the center rack in the oven and the pan of root vegetables beneath it. Roast for 25 to 30 minutes or until the squash and the root vegetables are tender and lightly browned around the edges.

5. Meanwhile, combine the orange juice, soy sauce, and sherry in a small dish. When the vegetables are done, drizzle the mixture over the root vegetables and stir to coat evenly. Roast them for about 2 more minutes. Season them with salt and pepper to taste.

6. Set each squash half on a plate, spoon the roasted vegetables into the center, and serve.

This is a perfect accompaniment to an autumn meal of roast pork or chicken. You'll use two oven racks for this recipe. To serve as a vegetarian main course, serve sautéed greens and steamed, herbed wild rice on the side. ■ Makes 4 servings

Pesto-Roasted Potatoes

3 tablespoons freshly grated Parmesan

2 tablespoons dried bread crumbs

1 tablespoon crushed dried basil

3/4 teaspoon kosher salt

3 tablespoons olive oil

2 garlic cloves, minced

**12 baby red or fingerling potatoes, halved, or
6 larger potatoes, quartered**

These crispy, flavorful potatoes, a tasty accompaniment to any meal, are simple and quick to prepare. ■ Makes 6 servings

1. Position the oven racks so that they are evenly spaced. Preheat the oven to convection roast at 450°F. Cover a shallow baking or roasting pan with foil and coat with nonstick spray.

2. In a small bowl, combine the Parmesan, bread crumbs, basil, and salt; set aside. In a large bowl, mix the olive oil and garlic; add the potatoes and toss to coat evenly. Add the cheese mixture to the potatoes and, using a rubber spatula, turn the potatoes until they are evenly coated with it.

3. Spread the potatoes in an even layer on the prepared pan and roast on the top or center oven rack for 20 to 25 minutes, until the potatoes are browned and tender. Serve hot.

Pepper-Roasted Ranch Potatoes

4 large baking potatoes, scrubbed and each cut
   lengthwise into 6 wedges
1 tablespoon olive oil
1 teaspoon kosher salt
$1/2$ to 1 teaspoon cracked black peppercorns

1. Position the oven racks so that they are evenly spaced, with the top rack about 5 inches from the top of the oven. Place a ridged cast-iron grill pan on the top shelf of the oven and preheat the oven to 500°F or the highest setting on your oven. Once preheated, set the oven to convection roast or convection broil at 500°F. Or cover a shallow-rimmed baking pan with foil and coat with nonstick spray and do not preheat the pan.

2. Toss the potatoes with the olive oil, salt, and pepper in a large bowl. Spread them skin side down in an even layer on the prepared pan and roast on the top rack for 15 to 20 minutes or until they are tender.

Roast the potatoes along with hamburgers, steaks, pork chops, boneless chicken breasts, or any other meat you choose. I use the highest oven setting, and they are done in about 15 minutes. Roast the potatoes in the center of the oven if that's all you are cooking. You can also roast three pans of potatoes at once, on evenly spaced oven racks if you're cooking for a crowd. If you are roasting meat, place it on the center or upper rack and roast the potatoes on a lower rack.

◼ Makes 4 servings

This is truly one of my favorite ways to cook tiny new potatoes. Sometimes when I buy a sack of potatoes, there will be a few larger ones, which I cut in half or in quarters to match the size of smaller 1- to 1$^{1}/_{2}$-inch potatoes. No need to peel the potatoes, just scrub them. ■ Makes 6 servings

Baby Red Potatoes with Rosemary and Garlic Butter

12 baby red potatoes, halved, or 6 larger potatoes, quartered

1 tablespoon olive oil

1 tablespoon butter, melted

2 garlic cloves, minced

1 tablespoon minced fresh rosemary

2 teaspoons fresh thyme

1 teaspoon kosher salt

$^{1}/_{2}$ teaspoon cracked black peppercorns

1. Position the oven racks so that they are evenly spaced. Preheat the oven to convection roast at 450°F. Cover a shallow-rimmed pan with foil and coat with nonstick spray.

2. In a large bowl, toss the potatoes with the olive oil, butter, garlic, rosemary, thyme, salt, and pepper. (The potatoes can be prepared to this point several hours in advance if they are not cut.)

3. Put them into the prepared pan, leaving a little space between each potato, and roast in the center of the oven for 20 minutes, until the potatoes are tender and browned.

Roasted Baby Red Potatoes with Mustard

Preheat the oven and prepare a baking pan as directed above. Combine $^{1}/_{4}$ cup Dijon mustard, 2 teaspoons paprika, 1 teaspoon ground cumin, 1 teaspoon chili powder, and $^{1}/_{8}$ teaspoon cayenne pepper in a large bowl. Add 12 scrubbed and halved baby red potatoes (or 6 scrubbed and quartered larger red potatoes) and toss to coat the potatoes evenly. Put the potatoes into the prepared pan, leaving a little space between each potato. Roast for 20 to 25 minutes, until browned and fork-tender.

Creamy Garlic Potatoes

2 pounds unpeeled red potatoes, scrubbed and cut
    into 1-inch cubes

1 teaspoon kosher salt

Freshly ground black pepper

2 to 3 tablespoons chopped fresh or crushed dried
    rosemary

3 to 4 cloves garlic, minced

2 cups heavy cream or undiluted evaporated milk
    (not condensed)

1. Position the oven racks so that they are evenly spaced. If you cook these potatoes along with meat or poultry, place a rack in the center for the meat and one below for the potatoes. Pre-heat the oven to convection roast at 300° to 325°F. Position the oven rack so that the potato dish will sit on the very bottom of the oven as it cooks.

2. Butter a shallow 1½- to 2-quart baking dish. Place the potatoes in an even layer in the baking dish. Sprinkle with the salt, pepper, rosemary, and garlic. Pour the cream over them.

3. Roast on the center or bottom rack for 60 to 75 minutes, until the potatoes are done.

Cook these irresistibly flavorful (and rich) potatoes along with a turkey or a roast, and though they will be done in about an hour, there's no harm in letting them bake an extra 15 to 20 minutes. If you are worried about calories, use the low-fat evaporated milk alternative.

■ Makes 6 to 8 servings

Try this for your
Thanksgiving menu,
roasted on the bottom
rack of the oven, along
with scalloped potatoes
or Creamy Garlic
Potatoes (page 144),
while the turkey roasts
on the rack above. If you
slice the potatoes ahead,
rinse them well in cold
water and drain to
prevent discoloring.

■ Makes 6 to 8 servings

Sweet Potatoes or Yams Roasted with Orange

2 pounds sweet potatoes or yams, peeled and sliced $1/4$ inch thick
1 teaspoon kosher salt
2 teaspoons freshly grated orange zest
$1^1/2$ cups freshly squeezed orange juice

1. Position the oven racks so that they are evenly spaced if you are roasting the vegetables alone. Position a rack in the bottom of the oven if you are roasting them with poultry or meat. Preheat the oven to convection roast at 300° to 325°F, depending on the temperature needed for the poultry or roast.

2. Butter a $1^1/2$- to 2-quart shallow casserole. Arrange the sweet potatoes in the casserole. Sprinkle with the salt and orange zest. Pour the orange juice over them. Cover with foil.

3. Roast on the center or bottom rack for $1^1/4$ to $1^1/2$ hours or until the potatoes are tender. Remove the foil during the last 15 minutes of roasting.

Salads

Salads like the classic salade niçoise and others that include cooked vegetables are simply better when the veggies are roasted rather than steamed. Potatoes that are roasted have a firm texture and a mellow, more concentrated flavor. Roasted beets are unusually sweet and make an exciting salad arranged on a mixture of greens, topped with crumbled feta. Because of the increased flavor in roasted vegetables, these salads use less oil.

Salads made with roasted ingredients make a satisfying main course for lunch or supper. They can also be served as a first course, and then the number of servings is doubled.

One thing to remember: Roast the freshest, firmest vegetables for your salads. As with all cooking, the best ingredients make the best eating.

Black Bean Salad with Roasted Corn

4 ears fresh corn

2 large sweet onions, diced

$1/2$ cup extra virgin olive oil

2 cups cooked or canned black beans, drained

2 tablespoons seeded and finely diced jalapeños

$1/4$ cup freshly squeezed lime juice

1 teaspoon ground cumin seeds

Kosher salt and freshly ground black pepper

$1/2$ cup finely chopped fresh cilantro

Not only do the colors sparkle in this salad, but the flavors do, too. Roasting fresh corn on the cob produces irresistibly sweet little morsels. This is wonderful with roasted fresh salmon.

■ Makes 6 servings

1. Position the oven racks so that they are evenly spaced. Preheat the oven to convection roast at 425°F. Cover a shallow-rimmed baking pan with foil.

2. Remove all the silk and all but one layer of husks from each ear of corn. Dip them in water to moisten. Pull the husks back over the corn and place on the baking sheet.

3. Toss the onions with 1 tablespoon of the olive oil and place them alongside the corn in an even layer. Roast on the center rack for 20 minutes, until the onions are lightly browned.

4. Put the onions in a mixing bowl. Scrape the corn off the ears—each ear will produce about $1/2$ cup corn—and add the corn to the onions. Add the black beans and jalapeños.

5. In a small bowl, combine the lime juice, cumin, and the remaining olive oil and whisk together until mixed. Add salt and pepper to taste. Pour the dressing into the corn and beans. Sprinkle with the cilantro. Cover and let stand for 30 minutes to an hour for the flavors to blend. If you make this a day in advance, cover it and re-frigerate. Bring to room temperature before serving.

Asian Chicken Salad

1 egg, beaten

$1/2$ cup milk

4 skinless, boneless chicken breast halves

$1/2$ cup all-purpose flour

1 cup finely chopped almonds

6 cups shredded fresh romaine leaves

2 cups finely shredded red cabbage

2 cups finely chopped napa cabbage

1 cup finely shredded carrots

4 green onions, thinly sliced on the diagonal

4 tablespoons sliced toasted almonds (see Note)

2 cups crisp chow mein noodles

Sesame Mustard Dressing (recipe follows)

1. Position the oven racks so that they are evenly spaced, with one rack in the center of the oven. Preheat the oven to convection bake at 500°F. Cover a rimless cookie sheet with foil and fold the edges under so it doesn't get blown loose while in the oven. Coat with nonstick spray.

2. Beat the egg and milk together in a shallow bowl. Dip the chicken in the milk mixture, roll in the flour, then dip again in the milk mixture. Roll in the chopped almonds to coat. Place the chicken on the cookie sheet and bake on the center rack for 10 minutes, until lightly browned and cooked through. Remove the chicken from the oven and cool.

Just as you would never find chow mein in China, I don't think you'd find this salad anywhere in Asia, but the concept is a popular one. In my version, chicken breasts are roasted, not deep-fried.

■ Makes 4 servings

3. Meanwhile, combine the romaine, red and napa cabbages, carrots, and green onions and divide them among four plates. Cut the chicken into $1/2$-inch diagonal slices and arrange on top of the greens. Sprinkle with the toasted almonds and noodles.

4. Serve with Sesame Mustard Dressing.

Sesame Mustard Dressing

In a medium bowl, whisk together $1/3$ cup honey, $1/3$ cup rice wine vinegar, $1/4$ cup mayonnaise, $1/4$ cup Dijon mustard, and 1 teaspoon sesame oil. Put in a bowl and serve.

Note: To toast almonds, spread them in an even layer on a cookie sheet and place in the oven as it preheats. Watch them carefully. The almonds will toast in 3 to 5 minutes.

> This salad is wonderful served warm or at room temperature with French bread and a green salad. ■ Makes 6 servings

Pasta Salad with Roasted Vegetables and Feta

1 red bell pepper, cored, seeded, and quartered lengthwise

1 yellow bell pepper, cored, seeded, and quartered lengthwise

1 medium eggplant, cut into 2-inch cubes (about 12 ounces)

1 medium zucchini, cut into $^1/_2$-inch slices

1 fresh tomato, halved crosswise

6 tablespoons olive oil

$^1/_4$ teaspoon kosher salt

$^1/_4$ teaspoon coarsely ground black pepper

$^1/_2$ cup drained and julienned sun-dried tomatoes (oil-packed)

$^1/_2$ cup arugula, torn in pieces

$^1/_2$ cup shredded fresh basil

2 tablespoons balsamic vinegar

2 tablespoons minced fresh garlic

8 ounces (half a box) farfalle (bowties) pasta, cooked and drained

4 ounces crumbled feta

1. Position the oven racks so that they are evenly spaced, with one rack in the center of the oven. Preheat the oven to convection roast at 450°F. Cover a shallow-rimmed pan with foil and coat with nonstick spray.

2. In a medium bowl, toss the peppers, eggplant, zucchini, and tomato with 2 tablespoons of the olive oil, the salt, and pepper. Arrange the peppers skin side up on the prepared pan. Place the tomato halves cut side down on the pan and scatter the eggplant and zucchini around them in an even layer.

3. Roast on the center rack for 15 minutes or just until the peppers are seared and the edges of the eggplant are browned. Remove from the oven. Peel the skins off the peppers, cut them into $^1/_2$-inch strips, and place them in a large bowl. Remove the skin from the tomato and chop the flesh; add to the peppers. Add the eggplant, zucchini, sun-dried tomatoes, arugula, basil, the remaining 4 tablespoons olive oil, vinegar, garlic, and cooked pasta. Toss to coat.

4. Put the mixture in a large shallow bowl or platter and sprinkle with the feta.

5. Serve immediately or at room temperature, or refrigerate for later use. Bring to room temperature before serving.

Roasted Red Potato Salad with Herb Vinaigrette

2 pounds small red potatoes, scrubbed and cut
   into 1-inch pieces

3 tablespoons olive oil

1 tablespoon chopped fresh rosemary

1 teaspoon kosher salt

Freshly ground black pepper

1 cup (about 1 bunch) thinly sliced green onions

1 cup diced celery

1 green bell pepper, seeded and diced

3 tablespoons Dijon mustard

3 tablespoons white balsamic vinegar or white
   wine vinegar

2 garlic cloves, minced

$1/2$ cup extra virgin olive oil

$1/4$ cup minced fresh flat-leaf parsley

1. Position the oven racks so that they are evenly spaced, with one rack in the center of the oven. Preheat the oven to convection roast at 425°F. Cover a baking sheet or shallow roasting pan with foil and coat with nonstick spray.

2. In a large bowl, toss the potatoes with the olive oil and rosemary. Spread in an even layer on the prepared roasting pan. Sprinkle with salt and pepper. Roast on the center rack for 15 to 20 minutes, turning once, until the potatoes are golden brown on the edges and fork-tender. Cool.

3. Return the potatoes to the large bowl and toss with the green onions, celery, and bell pepper until mixed.

4. Whisk together the mustard, vinegar, garlic, and extra virgin olive oil in a small bowl until well blended. Pour the dressing over the salad and toss to combine. Put in a serving dish and sprinkle with the parsley.

This is a break from potato salads dressed with mayonnaise, and much tastier!

■ Makes 6 servings

This is my version of the classic French salad I enjoyed time and again in Nice. Roasting concentrates the flavor of fresh green beans.

■ Makes 6 servings

Salade Niçoise

2 tablespoons extra virgin olive oil

2 garlic cloves, minced

1 teaspoon kosher salt

$^1/_2$ teaspoon coarsely ground black pepper

$1^1/_2$ pounds fresh tuna steaks (1 inch thick)

$1^1/_2$ pounds small red potatoes, scrubbed and cut into 1-inch cubes

1 pound fresh green beans, trimmed

1 pint grape or cherry tomatoes, halved

1 cup yellow cherry tomatoes, halved

1 head Boston or soft leaf lettuce, patted dry

4 hard-cooked eggs, peeled and quartered

12 pitted black olives such as Niçoise or Kalamata

Niçoise Dressing (recipe follows)

1. Position the oven racks so that they are evenly spaced, with one rack in the center of the oven. Preheat the oven to convection roast at 450°F. Line two rimmed baking sheets with foil and coat with nonstick spray.

2. Combine the olive oil, garlic, salt, and pepper in a mixing bowl.

3. Coat the tuna steaks with the oil mixture and place on one of the baking sheets. Toss the potatoes and green beans with the remaining oil mixture and spread them in an even layer over the second baking sheet.

4. Roast the tuna on the top rack for 5 to 6 minutes, turning once. Remove from the oven.

5. Roast the vegetables on the center or bottom racks for 15 to 20 minutes, until the potatoes are tender and the beans are lightly browned. Combine the roasted potatoes and beans with the red and yellow cherry tomatoes.

6. Line a salad bowl or individual salad plates with lettuce. Top with the roasted vegetables, eggs, and olives. Slice the tuna and fan it over the top of the salad. Drizzle with the dressing and serve.

Niçoise Dressing

■ Makes $3/4$ cup

1 tablespoon Dijon mustard
1 tablespoon balsamic or red wine vinegar
2 tablespoons freshly squeezed lemon juice
1 garlic clove, minced
Kosher salt and freshly ground black pepper to taste
$1/2$ cup olive oil
Fresh chives or flat-leaf parsley

1. Whisk all the ingredients, except for the olive oil and chives, together in a bowl. Add the olive oil in a thin stream, whisking until combined. Add the chives.

2. Drizzle the dressing over the salad.

Slow-Roasted Four-Grain Salad

$1/2$ cup wild rice, washed

$1/2$ cup whole wheat berries

$1/2$ cup whole rye berries

$1/2$ cup whole pearl barley

1 teaspoon kosher salt

$1/4$ cup olive oil

Juice of 1 lemon

2 cups chopped celery

2 cups finely diced seeded red bell peppers

1 cup finely chopped green onion

1 cup minced fresh flat-leaf parsley

$1/2$ cup minced fresh mint

Very slow roasting—175°F in a covered casserole—is ideal for whole-kernel grains as well as wild rice. The earthy flavors of whole grains blend well with the flavors we usually associate with another classic—tabbouleh.

■ Makes 12 servings

1. Position the oven racks so that the top rack is in the center of the oven. Set the oven to convection roast at 175°F. Combine the wild rice, wheat berries, rye berries, and barley in a heavy casserole with a tight-fitting lid. Add 4 cups water and the salt.

2. Cover the casserole and put it in the oven. Roast on the center rack for 5 hours, until all the water has been absorbed.

3. Remove from the oven and with a fork stir in the olive oil and lemon juice. Cool to room temperature. Put the grains into a serving bowl and add the celery, peppers, green onion, parsley, and mint.

4. Let the salad stand at room temperature for about 30 minutes to allow the flavors to blend.

Sweet potatoes are pale yellow, yams are deeper orange, and red garnets have a reddish hue. If you have trouble finding all three, just buy three pounds' worth of what you can find. This colorful salad is perfect with roast pork, or on the Thanksgiving menu as a refreshing change from the traditional sweet potato dishes. ■ Makes 6 to 8 servings

Sweet Potato, Red Garnet, and Yam Salad

3 pounds sweet potatoes, yams, and red garnets, peeled and cut into 1-inch pieces, rinsed and dried

1 tablespoon canola, vegetable, or olive oil

$1^1/2$ teaspoons kosher salt

1 tablespoon butter, softened

1 tablespoon minced fresh ginger

3 tablespoons frozen orange juice concentrate, thawed

4 slices thick-cut bacon, cut into 1-inch pieces

1 garlic clove, minced

$1/4$ cup freshly squeezed lemon juice

1 teaspoon freshly grated orange zest

$1/4$ cup minced fresh shallots

2 tablespoons chopped fresh chives

1. Position the oven racks so that they are evenly spaced. Preheat the oven to convection roast at 450°F. Cover a baking sheet with foil and coat with nonstick spray.

2. In a large bowl, toss the sweet potatoes, yams, and garnets with the canola oil. Sprinkle with the salt. Spread them in an even layer in the roasting pan.

3. Roast (on any rack) for 10 minutes. Add the butter, ginger, and orange juice. Toss to coat the potatoes evenly. Return to the oven and roast for 10 more minutes or until fork-tender.

4. While the potatoes finish roasting, cook the bacon in a large skillet until crisp. In a bowl, whisk together the garlic, lemon juice, orange zest, and shallots. Whisk in 2 tablespoons of bacon drippings and, while the potatoes are still warm, toss them in the dressing.

5. Put the potatoes in a serving bowl and top with the bacon and chives.

Yeast Breads

Bread baked in the convection oven browns evenly and retains a moist crumb. What's more, I can bake on as many as three levels at one time, depending on the height of the loaves, without having to switch loaves around in the oven partway through baking.

French bread and rustic breads bake wonderfully at a high temperature with moisture added to the oven. Circulating hot, moist air around the loaves makes the best crustiest rustic loaves and baguettes. A basic recipe for French bread with variations is included in this chapter along with a Rustic Round Loaf.

The moist, dense, dark peasant breads of Europe are among my favorites. Because these breads are dense and need more time for heat to penetrate to the center of the loaf, their baking temperature is reduced by 25 to 50 degrees, but baking times compared to those for a conventional oven are not reduced.

Many of our favorite bread recipes include sugar, eggs, and shortening, which cause the loaves to brown quickly. These breads must be baked at temperatures 25 to 50 degrees lower than conventional baking temperatures. For example, if your favorite recipe calls for the bread to be baked at 375°F, reduce the convection oven temperature to 350°F. Baking times will remain about the same or be reduced by 5 to 10 minutes.

To check for doneness in any of these breads, insert a long wooden skewer into the center of the loaf. If it comes out clean and dry, the bread is done. If the skewer "drags" upon removal, or if the skewer feels moist, then the loaf needs to bake a few more minutes. If the loaf is getting very dark and the center is still not done, lower the oven temperature by another 25 degrees for the remaining baking time and cover the loaf with a piece of foil crimped around the edges of the pan.

Guidelines for Baking Yeast Breads in a Convection Oven

The following guidelines will help you to convert your favorite yeast bread recipes to convection baking. The baking temperature is generally reduced for dense breads, while the time may remain the same or even be slightly longer to allow heat penetration. The results are worth the effort.

Type of Yeast Bread/ Size and Shape of Pan	Convection Bake Temperature	Time	Comments
Rustic, crusty loaves, round: shape, and allow to rise on dark, noninsulated, rimless cookie sheet	400°F or 450°F	20 to 22 minutes	To produce a crusty loaf with open interior texture, bake on preheated stone placed on the center rack of the oven; produce steam in oven for best results (see recipe).
Baguettes, crusty, elongated: shape, and allow to rise on dark, noninsulated, rimless cookie sheet	450°F	13 to 16 minutes	To produce a crusty loaf with open interior texture, bake on preheated stone or tiles placed in center of the oven; produce steam in oven for best results (see recipe).
Bread baked in loaf pan, or free-form round shape baked on rimmed or rimless cookie sheet	350°F	30 to 35 minutes	Insert long wooden skewer into center of loaf. When skewer comes out clean and dry, loaf is done. Bake in center of oven.
Bread with high sugar, egg, and milk content, such as sweet rolls, holiday breads; bake on parchment-covered rimless cookie sheet	300° to 325°F	30 to 35 minutes, until loaf tests done using a wooden skewer	Sugar, egg, and milk products cause breads to brown quickly; temperature needs to be reduced so that the center bakes before loaf is too dark. Bake in center of oven.

Type of Yeast Bread/ Size and Shape of Pan	Convection Bake Temperature	Time	Comments
Dinner rolls, hamburger buns: free-form on rimless sheet or baked in muffin tins	375°F	12 to 18 minutes	Check for doneness with wooden skewer; baking time may be slightly longer in a muffin tin. Bake in center of oven.
Caramel rolls: bake in individual muffin tins or in rectangular pan	325°F	25 to 30 minutes for muffin cups, or 40 to 45 minutes in rectangular pan	Rolls baked together in a rectangular pan take longer to bake; check center for doneness. Bake in center of oven.
Breadsticks: shape, and let rise on dark, noninsulated, rimless cookie sheet	400°F	15 to 20 minutes	Bake on rimless cookie sheet for best results. Can bake on any level at the same time on multiple cookie sheets.
Moist and dense loaves such as pumpernickel: bake free-form on rimless cookie sheet or in loaf pans	300°F	55 to 65 minutes	Dense loaves require a longer baking time because heat penetrates to the center slowly. Bake in center of oven.

If you're a home baker who is interested in making crusty French bread, you will be pleased with the results when you bake the bread in a convection oven. Remember it is also important to have steam in the oven. I keep a pan of river rocks on the bottom rack in my oven and preheat them right along with the oven itself. For added crustiness I place a baking stone or unglazed tiles on the center rack in the oven. The tiles help to maintain an even, hot heat and to stabilize the oven temperature. I place the loaves on a dark, noninsulated rimless cookie sheet. Spraying water on the rocks creates a burst of steam essential for creating a crusty crust.

■ Makes 3 loaves

Crusty French Bread

2¹/4 teaspoons (1 package) active dry yeast

2 teaspoons salt

4 cups bread flour

1. In a large bowl, dissolve the yeast in 1¹/2 cups warm (105° to 115°F) water. Let stand until the yeast bubbles. Stir in the salt and half the flour. Let stand for 5 minutes, until bubbly.

2. Stir in the rest of the flour a little at a time until a soft dough forms. If necessary, you may need to add more flour, a tablespoon at a time (depending on the climate: in warm, moist conditions, you'll need a bit more flour; in very dry, arid places, like Minnesota in the winter, you may need to add a bit more water).

3. Cover, and let the dough stand for 15 minutes until it begins to rise.

4. Turn out onto a very lightly floured board and knead until the dough is smooth and feels as if all the lumps of flour are gone.

5. Place in a lightly greased bowl, cover, and let rise until doubled, about an hour.

6. Divide the dough into three parts to make baguettes. Shape each into a long, narrow loaf. Place on a lightly greased, dark, rimless cookie sheet (not one that is insulated), with the smoothest side of the loaf up. Cover and let rise again for 45 minutes, until puffy.

7. Position the oven racks on the very bottom, the center, and the upper center of the oven. Place a rimmed cookie sheet filled with lake or river rocks on the very bottom level. Preheat the oven at 465°F (regular bake) for at least 20 minutes. Center a baking stone or 6 unglazed tiles on the center rack (place the tiles 1 to 2 inches apart for air circulation).

8. When the dough has risen until puffy, slash the loaves with a sharp, serrated knife diagonally across the top in three or four places, about ¹/4 inch deep. Reduce the oven temperature to convection bake at 450°F. Using a spray bottle filled with plain water, spritz the loaves generously. Pour ³/4 to 1 cup cool water into the pan of rocks beneath (a sport water bottle works well). *(continued)*

9. Bake on the center rack (on preheated tiles) for 15 minutes, until the loaves are browned and crusty. Remove the bread from the oven and cool on a wire rack.

ALTERNATE MIXING DIRECTIONS

BREAD MACHINE: Measure all the ingredients into the container of a bread machine and program the machine for the "dough" setting. When the dough is ready, continue with step 6.

FOOD PROCESSOR: Measure the yeast and dry ingredients into the container of a food processor fitted with a steel blade. Turn the processor on and slowly add the water through the feed tube; process until the dough is smooth and shiny and pulls away from the sides of the bowl. Cover, and let rise until the dough is doubled.

Sheaves of Wheat
After rising (step 8), snip the loaves with scissors at a 45-degree angle, pulling each snipped piece outward on opposite sides so that the loaves resemble sheaves of wheat.

Sun-Dried Tomato Baguettes
Soak $1/2$ cup julienned sun-dried tomatoes in hot water for 10 minutes. Drain well and pat dry.

Knead into the dough in step 4. Proceed as directed.

Kalamata Olive Loaf
Pit and chop $1/2$ cup well-drained Kalamata olives and add to the dough in step 4. Shape the dough into a round loaf and place on a lightly greased, dark, rimless (noninsulated) cookie sheet. Cover and let rise for 45 minutes, until puffy. Preheat the oven as directed in step 7. Before baking, slash the loaf diagonally with a serrated knife or razor blade across the top in three places. Bake at the temperature given in step 8 for 20 to 25 minutes or until crusty and browned. Cool on a wire rack.

Walnut-Fig Loaf
Chop $1/2$ cup walnuts and $1/2$ cup dried figs. Knead into the dough in step 4. Shape the dough into a round loaf and place on a lightly greased, dark, rimless (noninsulated) cookie sheet. Cover and let rise for 45 minutes, until puffy. Preheat the oven as directed in step 7. Before baking, slash the loaf diagonally with a serrated knife or razor blade across the top in three places. Bake at the temperature given in step 8 for 20 to 25 minutes or until crusty and browned. Cool on a wire rack.

Crusty Rustic Loaves

There are a few important things involved in getting a crusty baguette or a rustic bread to turn out perfectly:

1. First, the dough—it's a simple mixture of flour, salt, yeast, and water. It must be moist rather than dry and stiff. I've found that I can get beautiful results whether I mix the dough by hand, with a steel blade, in the food processor, or in the bread machine. The trick is to create a dough that is moist enough to form big bubbles inside so that the baked loaf has an open texture. Moistness also contributes to a crunchy, chewy crust.

2. The second important thing is to produce steam in the oven. I do this by preheating a pan of 1-inch rocks on the bottom shelf of the oven. I use a $12^1/2$ × $17^1/2$-inch rimmed pan filled with river rocks or landscape rocks. To create the steam, I squirt about a cupful of water onto the hot rocks, creating a burst of steam after I place the loaves in the oven.

3. Third, hot air in the convection oven circulates the heat and steam around the baking loaves to create a crunchy crust.

4. Rustic loaves require stabilized high heat. This can be accomplished by preheating tiles in the oven (on a rack in the center) to mimic a brick oven. The tiles help to maintain a high heat. Plain unglazed tiles from a flooring supply store work well. You can also place a baking stone into the oven if you have one. A kit called the "Hearthstone" kit works beautifully but is expensive. Because it is sometimes difficult and messy to transfer loaves directly onto preheated tiles or stones, I simply place the shaped loaves on a dark, noninsulated, rimless cookie sheet to rise and then set the cookie sheet right on the preheated tiles to bake.

5. If you do not have the pan of rocks or tiles, at least be sure to use a dark, noninsulated, rimless cookie sheet for baking the bread and spray the oven and risen loaves with plain water before and during baking. This does not produce as nice a crust as outlined in step 4 but is a good compromise.

This is the kind of loaf I like to have hot out of the oven to tear apart and dip in a brothy country-style soup. It's crusty with large, bubbly holes. For the best flavor, use the overnight method. For the fastest results follow the same-day method. Note that there are two different methods for baking the bread. The crustiest loaf is achieved with Baking Method #1. However, lacking the tiles and rocks, Baking Method #2 is a good alternative.

■ Makes 2 loaves

No-Knead Rustic Round Loaf

2 1/4 teaspoons (1 package) active dry yeast, plus
   1 teaspoon
5 to 6 cups unbleached bread flour
2 teaspoons salt

1. In a large glass, pottery, or hard plastic mixing bowl, mix 1 teaspoon of the yeast, 1 cup of tepid (95°F) water, and 1 cup of the flour. Cover with plastic wrap and let stand at room temperature for at least 5 hours or overnight, until bubbly.

2. Stir in the remaining package of yeast, 2 cups tepid water, and 2 cups of the flour along with the salt, and beat until the dough is smooth. Stir in the remaining 2 to 3 cups of flour until the dough pulls away from the sides of the bowl. With a large scraper or with your hand (oil your hands first), fold the dough over onto itself once or twice to make a smooth ball.

3. Cover the bowl tightly with plastic wrap and let the dough rise in a warm place until doubled in volume, about 40 minutes. The dough should be shiny and contain big bubbles. Fold the dough over onto itself again, cover, and let it rise once more for 40 minutes.

4. Dust a work surface with flour. Turn the dough out onto the surface, being careful not to deflate the air bubbles. With a pair of scissors, cut the dough in half.

5. Gently shape each half into a round loaf and transfer each onto one of two lightly greased, dark, noninsulated cookie sheets. Let them rise for 40 minutes or until puffy. With a sharp, serrated knife, make three diagonal slashes across the top of each loaf, about $1/4$ inch deep, cutting at a 45-degree angle. Bake the loaves one at a time if using Baking Method #1, or bake both pans at the same time if using Baking Method #2.

6. BAKING METHOD #1: Position the oven racks on the very bottom and in the center of the oven. Place a rimmed cookie sheet filled with lake or river rocks on the very bottom level. Center a baking stone or 6 unglazed tiles on the rack (place the tiles 1 to 2 inches away from the sides of the oven for air circulation). Preheat the oven at 465°F (regular bake) for at least 20 minutes. Reset the oven to convection bake at 400°F.

7. Using a spray bottle filled with plain water, spritz the loaf generously. Place the loaf on top of the stone in the oven. Pour $3/4$ to 1 cup cool water into the pan of rocks beneath (a sport water bottle works well). Bake for 20 to 25 minutes, until the loaf is shiny and crusty.

8. BAKING METHOD #2: With this method you can bake two to three pans of bread at one time. Position the oven racks so that they are equally spaced, with the second rack in the center of the oven. Preheat the oven to convection bake at 450°F.

9. Shape the loaves and let them rise as in step 5. Using a spray bottle filled with water, spritz the loaves generously. Reduce the temperature to 400°F and bake for 20 to 25 minutes, until golden and crusty. Remove the bread from the oven and cool on a wire rack.

Rosemary Breadsticks

2^1/4 teaspoons (1 package) active dry yeast

2^1/2 cups unbleached all-purpose flour

1 teaspoon salt

2 tablespoons olive oil, plus more for brushing
breadsticks

3 tablespoons finely chopped fresh rosemary

1. Pour ^{1}/2 cup warm (105° to 115°F) water into the bowl of a food processor fitted with the steel blade. Add the yeast and mix. Let stand for 5 minutes, until the yeast begins to foam.

2. Measure the flour, salt, olive oil, and rosemary into the bowl. Turn the processor on and add about ^{1}/2 cup warm water through the feed tube to make a soft dough. Let the dough rise until doubled, 1 to 2 hours. Oil three dark, noninsulated rimless cookie sheets.

3. Sprinkle a work surface with flour and turn the dough out onto it. Pat it into a rectangular shape about 6 inches wide and 12 inches long.

4. With the straight edge of a knife, cut across the short side of the dough to make 16 slices.

5. Roll each into a long, thin breadstick. Cut each crosswise into two breadsticks. Arrange them on the cookie sheets and let rise until puffy, about 20 minutes. Brush them with olive oil.

6. Position the oven racks so that they are evenly spaced. Preheat the oven to convection bake at 400°F. Bake the breadsticks for 15 to 20 minutes, until lightly golden and crisp. Transfer them to a wire rack to cool.

These breadsticks bake to golden crispness in the convection oven, and are a fun project to do with kids.

■ Makes 32 breadsticks

Perfect for sandwiches, toast in the morning, or the evening bread basket, this bread is a basic in a home bread baker's repertoire. I prefer to bake it in free-form rounds, but it is just as good baked in a loaf pan. ■ Makes one large round loaf or two 9 × 5-inch loaves

Classic White Bread

$2^{1}/4$ teaspoons (1 package) active dry yeast

2 teaspoons sugar

2 cups milk, scalded and cooled to 105° to 115°F

2 teaspoons salt

2 tablespoons melted butter

5 to $5^{1}/2$ cups unbleached bread or all-purpose flour

1. In a large warmed bowl, dissolve the yeast and sugar in $^{1}/4$ cup warm (105° to 115°F) water. Let stand for about 5 minutes or until the yeast foams.

2. Add the milk, salt, and melted butter. Beat in 2 cups of the flour until smooth. Add enough of the remaining flour to make a stiff dough. Cover the bowl and let the dough rest for 15 minutes.

3. Turn the dough out onto a lightly floured board. Knead, adding flour sparingly, until the dough is smooth and springy, about 10 minutes.

If desired, you may mix and knead the dough in a heavy-duty mixer using the dough hook.

4. Cover and let rise until doubled, 1 to $1^{1}/2$ hours. Punch the dough down. Turn it out onto a lightly oiled board. Knead to squeeze out air bubbles. Shape into one large round loaf and place on a lightly greased baking sheet, or divide the dough into two pieces and shape into two oblong loaves. Grease two 9 × 5-inch loaf pans. Place the loaves into the pans smooth side up. Cover and let rise until almost doubled, 45 minutes to 1 hour.

5. Position the oven racks so that the top rack is in the center of the oven. Preheat the oven to convection bake at 350°F. Bake on the center rack for 25 to 30 minutes or until a wooden skewer inserted into the bread comes out clean and dry. Remove the bread from the pans and cool on a wire rack.

This is a favorite bread, especially in the Midwest, where many people have Scandinavian roots. ■ Makes two 9 x 5-inch loaves

Swedish Rye Bread

2 teaspoons each caraway seeds, anise seed, and
   fennel seeds
Freshly grated zest of 1 orange
2 cups milk, scalded and cooled to 105° to 115°F
2¹/4 teaspoons (1 package) active dry yeast
¹/4 cup dark molasses
2 teaspoons salt
2 tablespoons butter, melted
2 cups medium rye flour
3 to 3¹/2 cups unbleached bread flour (wheat)

1. Grind the caraway seeds, anise seed, and fennel seeds in a mortar and pestle or a spice or coffee grinder and place in a large bowl with the orange zest and milk.

2. In a large warmed bowl, mix the yeast and molasses with ¹/4 cup warm (105° to 115°F) water. Let stand about 5 minutes or until the yeast foams. Add the milk mixture, salt, and melted butter. Beat in the rye flour until smooth. Beat in enough bread flour to make a stiff dough. Cover the bowl and let the dough rest for 15 minutes.

3. Turn the dough out onto a lightly floured board. Knead, adding flour sparingly until the dough is smooth and springy, about 10 minutes. If desired, you may mix and knead the dough in a heavy-duty mixer using the dough hook.

4. Cover and let rise until doubled, 1 to 1¹/2 hours. Punch the dough down. Turn it out onto a lightly oiled board. Knead to squeeze out air bubbles. Divide the dough into two pieces and shape into two oblong loaves. Grease two 9 x 5-inch loaf pans. Place the loaves in the pans smooth side up. Cover and let rise until almost doubled, 45 minutes to 1 hour.

5. Position the oven racks so that the top rack is in the center of the oven. Preheat the oven to convection bake at 325°F. Bake on the center rack for 25 to 30 minutes or until a wooden skewer inserted into the bread comes out clean and dry. Remove the bread from the pans and cool on a wire rack.

Honey Whole Wheat Bread

2^1/4 teaspoons (1 package) active dry yeast

^{1}/4 cup honey

2 tablespoons butter, melted

1^1/2 cups milk, scalded and cooled to 105° to 115°F

2 eggs, at room temperature

2 cups whole wheat flour

3 to 3^1/2 cups bread flour

1. In a large, warmed bowl, dissolve the yeast in ^{1}/4 cup warm (105° to 115°F) water. Add the honey. Let stand for 5 minutes or until the yeast foams.

2. Add the melted butter, milk, eggs, and whole wheat flour and mix until smooth. Beat in enough of the bread flour to make a stiff dough. Cover the bowl and let the dough rest for 15 minutes.

3. Turn the dough out onto a lightly floured board. Knead, adding flour sparingly, until the dough is springy and smooth, about 10 minutes. If desired, you may mix and knead the dough in a heavy-duty mixer using the dough hook.

4. Cover and let rise until doubled, 1 to 1^1/2 hours. Punch the dough down. Turn it out onto a lightly oiled board. Knead to squeeze out air bubbles. Divide the dough into two pieces and shape into two oblong loaves. Grease two 9 × 5-inch loaf pans. Place the loaves in the pans smooth side up. Cover and let rise until almost doubled, 45 minutes to 1 hour.

5. Position the oven racks so that the top rack is in the center of the oven. Preheat the oven to convection bake at 325°F. Bake on the center rack for 25 to 30 minutes or until a wooden skewer inserted into the bread comes out clean and dry. Remove the bread from the pans and cool on a wire rack.

Here's another favorite country bread that includes honey and eggs. The baking temperature is reduced in the convection oven although the baking time remains the same.

■ Makes two 9 × 5-inch loaves

Cinnamon-Raisin Bread with Walnuts

2^1/4 teaspoons (1 package) active dry yeast

4 tablespoons packed brown sugar

1^1/2 teaspoons ground cinnamon

1^1/2 teaspoons salt

2 tablespoons butter, softened

2 cups whole wheat flour

2 cups bread flour

^{3}/4 cup raisins

^{3}/4 cup chopped walnuts or pecans

1. Pour 1^1/2 cups warm (105° to 115°F) water into a large warmed mixing bowl. Add the yeast and sugar; stir and let stand for 5 minutes, until the yeast begins to bubble.

2. Add the cinnamon, salt, butter, and whole wheat flour. Beat until smooth. Stir in 1 cup bread flour and mix until blended. Cover and let stand for 15 minutes.

3. Stir in the remaining 1 cup bread flour to make a smooth dough. Turn the dough out onto a lightly floured board and knead, adding flour if necessary, for about 5 minutes, until smooth and springy. Knead in the raisins and nuts.

4. Wash the bowl, grease it, and place the dough back in the bowl. Turn it over to grease the top. Cover and let it rise until doubled, about 1 hour.

5. Shape into a smooth round loaf and place smooth side up onto a lightly greased rimless baking sheet. Cover and let rise in a warm place for 45 to 60 minutes or until almost doubled.

6. Position the oven racks so that the top rack is in the center of the oven. Preheat the oven to convection bake at 325°F. Bake on the center rack of the oven for 30 to 35 minutes or until a wooden skewer inserted into the center of the bread comes out clean and dry. Remove the bread from the baking sheet and cool on a wire rack.

Cinnamon perfumes the air as this loaf bakes. This not-too-sweet wheat bread is a perfect match for aged sharp Cheddar. This dense loaf bakes beautifully in the convection oven at a lower temperature than you'd expect. ■ Makes 1 round loaf

This light-textured loaf is showy in a buffet. This is a batter bread, easy to stir up, no kneading involved. It bakes quickly in the convection oven. ■ Makes 1 loaf

Sesame Egg Braid

1 egg, lightly beaten
2^1/$_2$ to 2^3/$_4$ cups unbleached all-purpose flour
2 tablespoons sugar
2^1/$_4$ teaspoons (1 package) active dry yeast
^{1}/$_2$ teaspoon salt
2 tablespoons canola oil or melted butter
1 tablespoon sesame seeds

1. In a small bowl, beat the egg with 1 cup warm (105° to 115°F) water. Reserve 1 tablespoon of the mixture and refrigerate. Pour the remaining mixture into a large mixing bowl.

2. Add 1^1/$_2$ cups of the flour, the sugar, yeast, salt, and oil. Beat with a wooden spoon until smooth, about 2 minutes. Stir in enough of the remaining flour just until a soft dough forms that will hold together in a soft, shiny mass.

3. Cover and let rise for about 1 hour or until doubled in size.

4. Turn the dough out onto a floured surface and pat it into a 12 × 6-inch rectangle. Cut it into three long pieces and roll each piece into a rounded strand. Braid the strands together to make a loaf. Lightly grease a dark, rimless, non-insulated baking sheet and place the loaf on the sheet.

5. Cover and let rise for about 1 hour or until almost doubled.

6. Position the oven racks so that they are evenly spaced. Preheat the oven to convection bake at 375°F. Brush the braid with the reserved egg mixture and sprinkle with sesame seeds.

7. Bake the bread on the center rack for 15 to 18 minutes or until golden brown and a wooden skewer inserted into the center of the loaf comes out clean and dry. Remove the bread from the oven and cool on a wire rack.

European-Style Whole Grain Breads

The moist, dense, dark peasant breads of Europe are among my favorites. These breads have heft. Slice them thinly and serve with equally flavorful cheese and slices of fresh pears, figs, or crisp apples.

Dense breads such as these need to be baked at a lower temperature than rustic breads and country-style breads. It takes time for the heat to penetrate the loaf. I often place a shallow pan of water in the bottom of the oven to add humidity as the bread bakes. Convection baking is ideal as it mimics the old European hearth, which produced natural circulation of air around the bread as it baked. The baking temperature is from 25 to 50 degrees lower than in a regular oven. The baking time is about the same as for conventional cooking.

This simple, wholesome bread is made with stone-ground rye flour. Baked in the convection oven, the crust is chewy and flavorful. It is not as dense a bread as others in this category, therefore it bakes at a slightly higher temperature. This is the bread we baked in the oven of the woodstove when I was growing up on the farm in northern Minnesota. The wood oven creates heat that circulates much like that of a convection oven. I have finally been able to bake bread that closely resembles my childhood favorite!

■ Makes 1 loaf

Farmer Rye Bread

2¹/4 teaspoons (1 package) active dry yeast
1 teaspoon salt
1 tablespoon brown sugar or light molasses
1 cup stone-ground rye flour
2¹/3 cups unbleached bread flour

1. *To mix the dough in a bowl by hand,* measure 1¹/2 cups warm (105° to 115°F) water into a large mixing bowl. Add the yeast, salt, sugar, and rye flour. Beat until smooth. Slowly beat in the bread flour to make a stiff dough. Cover and let rest for 15 minutes. Turn it out onto a floured board and knead until the dough forms a smooth, nonsticky ball. Place in a lightly greased bowl, cover, and let rise for 1 hour or until doubled. Proceed with step 4.

2. *To mix the dough in a bread machine,* measure all of the ingredients into the work bowl, starting with the water. Program the machine to make dough. Proceed with step 4.

3. *To mix the dough in a food processor,* measure the flours, sugar, salt, and yeast into the bowl of a food processor fitted with the steel blade. Turn the processor on and add the water slowly through the feed tube, processing until the dough spins around the bowl in a solid but sticky mass. Leave the cover on the food processor and let the dough rise until it fills the bowl.

4. Turn it out onto a lightly floured board and shape it into a round loaf. Place on a lightly greased rimless cookie sheet. Cover and let rise for 45 minutes to 1 hour or until almost doubled.

5. Position the oven racks so that the top rack is in the center of the oven. Preheat the oven to convection bake at 350°F. Brush the loaf with water. Bake in the center of the oven for 30 to 35 minutes or until nicely browned and a wooden skewer inserted into the center of the loaf comes out clean and dry. Remove the bread from the oven and cool on a wire rack.

Scandinavian-Style Pumpernickel

4$\frac{1}{2}$ teaspoons (2 packages) active dry yeast

$\frac{1}{2}$ cup dark molasses

3 tablespoons butter, melted

2 tablespoons caraway seeds

1 teaspoon salt

2 cups rye meal, cracked wheat, or multigrain
  cereal

3 to 4 cups unbleached bread flour

1. In a large bowl, stir the yeast into 1$\frac{1}{2}$ cups warm (105° to 115°F) water; let stand for 5 minutes to soften. Add the molasses, butter, caraway seeds, and salt.

2. Stir in the rye meal. Let stand for 15 minutes. Stir in the bread flour 1 cup at a time. Beat in enough flour to make a stiff dough. Turn the dough out onto a lightly floured board. Cover with a cloth and let stand for 5 to 15 minutes.

3. Wash and grease the bowl; set aside. Sprinkle the work surface with flour and knead the dough until smooth, 5 to 10 minutes. Place in the greased bowl, turning to grease all sides. Cover and let rise in a warm place until doubled, about 2 hours.

4. Punch the dough down. Divide in half. Shape each half into a loaf. Grease two 9 × 5-inch loaf pans and place the loaves in the pans smooth side up.

5. Cover and let the dough rise until almost doubled, 45 minutes to 1 hour.

6. Position the oven racks so that the top rack is in the center of the oven. Place a shallow pan of water on the very bottom rack in the oven. Preheat the oven to convection bake at 325°F for at least 20 minutes.

7. Fill a spray bottle with water and spray the loaves with water. Place on the center rack in the oven. Bake for 35 to 40 minutes or until a wooden skewer inserted into the center of each loaf comes out clean and dry. Turn the bread out of the pans; cool on a wire rack.

This bread is close-textured, grainy, and full of hearty flavor. It slices most easily the day after it is baked. Serve it very thinly sliced with a flavorful cheese such as gjetost, Jarlsberg, or Danish Havarti. ■ Makes 2 loaves

This is an easy refrigerator dough method, which requires no kneading. Once refrigerated for 2 to 24 hours, it is easy to shape and bake a number of different ways. These breads are rich with special ingredients, which will all brown quickly while baking. So, the baking temperature must be lower than that of conventional ovens while the baking time remains about the same. You'll be delighted with the moist crumb; because the crust is formed early in the baking, it locks in moisture.

■ Makes dough for 3 loaves, 24 sticky buns, or 12 giant sticky buns

Basic Sweet Dough for Yeast Coffee Cakes and Rolls

4^1/2 teaspoons (2 packages) active dry yeast
1 cup milk, scalded and cooled to 105° to 115°F
8 tablespoons (1 stick) butter, melted
^{1}/2 cup sugar
3 eggs
1 teaspoon salt
5 to 5^1/4 cups all-purpose flour

1. In a large bowl, combine the yeast and ^{1}/2 cup warm (105° to 115°F) water; stir. Let stand for 5 minutes or until the yeast foams. Stir in the milk, butter, sugar, eggs, and salt. Stir in the flour, 1 cup at a time, until the dough clings to-

gether in a mass but is still soft and sticky (see Note). (This may be before all of the flour is added.) Cover and refrigerate for 2 to 24 hours or up to 4 days.

2. Proceed as directed in one of the variations that follow.

Note: If you are in doubt as to whether you have added enough flour, keep in mind that it is better for the dough to be a little too wet than a little too dry.

Baking temperature is reduced when baking these gooey rolls, but the baking time remains about the same as in a conventional oven. The advantage of convection? The rolls are moist and delicious, not doughy.

■ Makes 24 rolls

Caramel-Pecan Sticky Rolls

Basic Sweet Dough (page 177)

FOR THE FILLING

$1/2$ pound (2 sticks) butter, softened

$3/4$ cup granulated sugar

2 teaspoons ground cinnamon

$1^1/2$ cups packed brown sugar

$1^1/2$ cups dark corn syrup or maple syrup

$1^1/2$ cups chopped pecans

1. Prepare the Basic Sweet Dough. Coat two 9-inch round or square pans with nonstick spray. Set aside.

2. Turn the dough out onto a lightly floured board and cut in half. Roll the chilled dough to make two 12-inch squares. To make the filling, spread each square with $1/2$ cup softened butter. Mix the granulated sugar and cinnamon and sprinkle each square with half of the cinnamon-sugar mixture. Roll each square up, jelly-roll style. Cut each roll into 12 equal pieces. This is easily done using a string.

3. Coat 24 muffin tins with nonstick spray. Place 1 tablespoon brown sugar, 1 tablespoon corn syrup, and 1 tablespoon chopped pecans into each cup. Place the dough pieces cut side down into each cup. Cover and let rise for about 1 hour, until doubled.

4. Position the oven racks so that they are evenly spaced. Preheat the oven to convection bake at 325°F. Bake the rolls on the center rack for 25 to 30 minutes or until golden brown. Invert onto a serving tray while still warm.

Swiss Onion Dinner Rolls

Basic Sweet Dough (page 177)

FOR THE FILLING

2 tablespoons butter

2 cups chopped onions

$1/2$ teaspoon ground or freshly grated nutmeg

$1/2$ cup freshly grated Parmesan

2 cups (8 ounces) shredded Swiss cheese

These cheesy rolls loaded with onions only need a green salad to make a terrific light lunch or dinner.

■ Makes 24 rolls

1. Prepare the Basic Sweet Dough. Cover and refrigerate for 2 to 24 hours or up to 4 days.

2. In a medium skillet, melt the butter, add the onions and nutmeg, and sauté until the onions are soft, 5 to 7 minutes. Grease 24 muffin tins and set aside.

3. Divide the refrigerated dough in half and roll each into a rectangle that is $1/2$ inch thick (about 12 × 16 inches). Spread each rectangle with $1/4$ cup of the Parmesan, 1 cup of the

Swiss cheese, and $1/2$ of the onion mixture. Roll each rectangle from the long end. Seal the seam and cut into 1-inch pieces. Place them cut side down into the greased muffin tins; cover loosely with plastic wrap and allow to rise for 45 minutes to 1 hour or until about doubled.

4. Position the oven racks so that they are evenly spaced. Preheat the oven to convection bake at 375°F. Bake on the center rack for 15 to 20 minutes, until golden brown. Remove the rolls from the tins and cool on a wire rack.

This is a special bread/cake that Danes like to make for the holiday season. It's a quick version of flaky Danish pastry.

■ Makes 16 servings

Danish Almond Kringle

2^1/4 teaspoons (1 package) active dry yeast

1 tablespoon sugar

^{1}/2 cup warm milk, 105° to 115°F

1 cup heavy cream, at room temperature

3^1/2 cups all-purpose flour

^{1}/4 cup sugar

1 teaspoon salt

1 teaspoon freshly ground cardamom (see Note)

8 tablespoons (1 stick) chilled unsalted butter, cut into slices

FOR THE ALMOND FILLING

One 8-ounce package almond paste (about 1 cup)

^{1}/2 cup chopped blanched almonds

^{1}/3 cup sugar

1 teaspoon ground cinnamon

1 teaspoon almond extract

FOR THE TOPPING

^{1}/3 cup sugar

1 egg white, beaten

^{1}/4 cup sliced almonds

1. In a small bowl, combine the yeast, sugar, and milk. Let stand until the yeast dissolves and begins to foam, about 10 minutes. Stir in the cream.

2. In a large bowl, combine the flour, sugar, salt, and cardamom. Cut in the butter until the mixture resembles coarse meal. Fold in the yeast mixture just until the dough is moistened. Cover and refrigerate for 12 to 24 hours.

3. Turn the chilled dough out onto a lightly floured surface. With a rolling pin, pound the dough until flattened to a 2-inch thickness, then roll the dough out into a 24-inch square.

4. To prepare the filling, blend the almond paste, almonds, sugar, cinnamon, and almond extract together. Spread the filling to within 1 inch of the edges of the square, and roll the dough up as tightly as possible.

5. Sprinkle the sugar for the topping on the work surface. Roll the dough firmly into the sugar to coat it well, and, at the same time, stretch it to form a log of dough 36 to 40 inches long.

6. Cover a baking sheet with parchment paper. Place the roll on the paper in the shape of a pretzel. Brush the surface with the egg white and sprinkle with the almonds. Cover and let rise for 45 minutes, or until puffy but not doubled.

7. Position the oven racks so that they are evenly spaced. Preheat the oven to convection bake at 300°F. Bake in the center of the oven for 30 to 35 minutes, until golden. Remove the bread from the oven and cool on a wire rack.

Note: White cardamom pods are generally used in Scandinavian cooking. Store-bought ground cardamom has very little flavor. It's best to grind the black seeds (removed from the pods) yourself using a mortar and pestle or a spice or coffee grinder.

Quick Breads

As with yeast breads, quick breads baked in the convection oven in the "convection bake" mode brown evenly and retain moisture. Although the baking temperature isn't always reduced, the baking time almost certainly will be. You can also bake quick breads on as many as three racks at one time without changing the time or temperature.

The sweeter and richer the quick bread, the lower the oven temperature needs to be to prevent overbrowning before the center is done. Use the recipes in this chapter and the chart as guides to convert your favorite recipes to convection baking.

Test for doneness by inserting a wooden skewer or toothpick into the center of the loaf. If it comes out clean and dry, the bread is done. If the loaf has browned before the center is done, lower the temperature 25 to 50 degrees and finish baking. You may want to keep notes for future reference, as ovens vary.

Guidelines for Baking Quick Breads in a Convection Oven

The following guidelines will help you to convert your favorite quick bread recipes to convection baking. You can use the recipes that follow as guidelines, too.

Type of Quick Bread/ Size and Shape of Pan	Convection Bake Temperature	Time	Comments
Muffins	400°F	15 to 16 minutes 15 to 18 minutes if recipe includes more sugar than given in basic recipe that follows	Baking temperature is not reduced, but baking time is, to produce moist, well-browned muffins.
Biscuits	400°F	10 to 12 minutes	Baking temperature not reduced, baking time is reduced for moist and tender biscuits.
Scones	350°F	15 to 20 minutes	Baking temperature reduced because of sugar content in scones.
Popovers	450°F then reduce to 300°F	10 minutes, then for 30 minutes. Popovers may also be baked at 325°F along with a roast, for 55 to 60 minutes	Baking temperature can vary according to your needs: at high temperature will brown quickly; lower temperature needed to cook the interior of the popovers.

Type of Quick Bread/ Size and Shape of Pan	Convection Bake Temperature	Time	Comments
Refrigerated crescent rolls	350°F	10 minutes; for large size, 15 minutes	Baking temperature not reduced, but baking time is reduced by one-third.
Quick bread ($9^1/2 \times 5^1/2$-inch loaf pan)	325°F	50 to 55 minutes	Baking temperature set 50 degrees lower than standard oven baking; time is slightly less.
Quick bread ($5^3/4 \times 3^1/2$-inch loaf pan)	350°F	35 to 45 minutes	Baking temperature set 25 degrees lower than standard oven.
Coffee cakes (fluted tube pan or springform pan)	325°F	55 to 60 minutes	Baking temperature set 25 degrees lower than standard oven.
Coffee cakes (13 × 9-inch pan)	325°F	40 to 45 minutes	Baking temperature set 25 degrees lower than standard oven.

Muffins used to be a healthy breakfast option, but in recent years they have become jumbo sources of fats and sugar. There's no reason why a medium muffin shouldn't be a reliable breakfast staple. Here's a basic recipe that's relatively low in butter and sugar but still completely satisfying. Once you master (and memorize) the basic formula, you can create anything you desire. Six variations follow. Rather than reduce the oven temperature here, I prefer to keep it the same as in the conventional oven, but reduce the baking time so you can bake them even on a workday morning.

■ Makes 12 muffins

Breakfast Muffins

2 cups all-purpose flour
$1/3$ cup sugar
1 tablespoon baking powder
$1/2$ teaspoon salt
6 tablespoons butter, softened
1 egg
1 cup milk

1. Position the oven racks so that they are evenly spaced. Preheat the oven to convection bake at 400°F. Grease 12 medium muffin cups or line with paper cupcake liners. If you use the cupcake liners, coat them with nonstick spray for easy removal of the muffins.

2. In a large bowl, mix the flour, sugar, baking powder, and salt. Add the butter, egg, and milk. Stir with a fork just until the ingredients are blended. (Overmixing will make the muffins bake into peaks with "tunnels" going from top to bottom.)

3. Fill the muffin cups two-thirds full. Bake in the center of the oven for 15 to 18 minutes or until golden and a wooden skewer inserted into the center of a muffin comes out clean. Serve hot.

Whole Wheat Muffins

Substitute 1 cup whole wheat flour for 1 cup all-purpose flour and substitute $1/3$ cup honey for the sugar.

Sour Cream Muffins

Use only 2 teaspoons baking powder and add $1/2$ teaspoon baking soda. Substitute dairy sour cream for the milk, mixed with 2 eggs instead of one.

Blueberry Muffins

Increase the sugar to $1/2$ cup. When all the ingredients are blended, carefully fold in $1^1/2$ cups fresh or frozen blueberries.

Honey Orange Muffins

Use 2 eggs. In the bottom of each muffin cup, place 1 teaspoon honey and 1 thin slice unpeeled orange cut into quarters. Spoon the batter on top.

Apple Muffins

Increase the sugar to $1/2$ cup. Add $1/2$ teaspoon ground cinnamon to the flour mixture. Add 1 cup shredded raw tart apple along with the butter. Sprinkle the tops with a mixture of $1/3$ cup packed brown sugar, $1/3$ cup chopped walnuts, and $1/2$ teaspoon ground cinnamon.

Date and Nut Muffins

Add 1 cup each finely chopped dates and finely chopped walnuts or pecans to the flour mixture before adding the liquid.

Buttermilk Biscuits

2 cups all-purpose flour

2 teaspoons sugar

$^1/_2$ teaspoon salt

2 teaspoons baking powder

$^1/_2$ teaspoon baking soda

5 tablespoons cold unsalted butter, cut into pieces

1 egg, lightly beaten

$^1/_2$ to $^2/_3$ cup buttermilk

Biscuits have been an American favorite since the early 1800s. Anything so well known has as many variations as there are enthusiasts. My favorite recipe includes an egg for lightness. As expected, when they're baked in the convection oven, they bake more quickly at a lower temperature. ■ Makes 12 biscuits

1. Position the oven racks so that they are evenly spaced. Preheat the oven to convection bake at 400°F.

2. In a medium bowl, mix the flour, sugar, salt, baking powder, and baking soda. Cut in the butter until the mixture resembles coarse crumbs.

3. Stir the egg and $^1/_2$ cup buttermilk together in a small bowl until blended. Pour the liquids over the dry ingredients, and stir with a fork just until the dry ingredients are moistened, adding a few more tablespoons of buttermilk if the mixture seems dry.

4. Turn the dough out onto a lightly floured surface. With floured hands, pat the dough out to a $1^1/_2$-inch thickness. Cut out rounds with a $2^1/_2$-inch cutter and place them on an ungreased baking sheet. Brush the tops of the biscuits with a bit of buttermilk. Dust with flour.

5. Bake in the center of the oven for 10 to 12 minutes, until the biscuits are golden brown. Serve immediately.

Cheddar Biscuits

Add 2 cups shredded Cheddar to the dry ingredients after cutting in the butter and before adding the liquid ingredients.

There isn't much difference in baking time between convection and regular ovens when you bake scones, only 5 to 10 minutes. The difference is in the wonderful texture, moist tender crumb, and golden, delicate crust that you can expect from the convection oven.

■ Makes 8 scones

Cream Scones with Currants and Orange

2 cups all-purpose flour

$1/4$ cup sugar

3 teaspoons baking powder

$1/2$ teaspoon salt

8 tablespoons (1 stick) cold butter, cut into small pieces

$1/2$ cup currants

1 egg

$1/2$ cup heavy cream

1 tablespoon freshly grated orange zest

1. Position the oven racks so that they are evenly spaced. Preheat the oven to convection bake at 350°F. Cover a rimless cookie sheet with parchment paper.

2. In the bowl of a food processor fitted with the steel blade, combine the flour, sugar, baking powder, and salt and pulse to combine. Add the butter and pulse on/off until the mixture resembles pea-sized crumbs.

3. Transfer the dough to a large bowl, add the currants, and stir to mix. In a small bowl, whisk together the egg, cream, and orange zest until blended and add to the flour mixture. *(continued)*

4. Stir with a fork until the dough makes moist clumps. Turn out onto a lightly floured surface and press together with your hands until the dough comes together.

5. Place the dough on the cookie sheet and pat into an 8-inch round about $3/4$ inch thick. Score into 8 equal-sized wedges using the straight edge of a knife, cutting all the way through the dough, but leaving the wedges in place.

6. Bake on the center rack until golden, 15 to 20 minutes.

Lemon-Raisin Scones

Substitute $1/2$ cup golden raisins for the currants and 1 tablespoon freshly grated lemon zest for the orange zest.

Cranberry-Tangerine Scones

Substitute $1/2$ cup dried cranberries for the currants and 1 tablespoon freshly grated tangerine zest for the orange zest.

Almond-Cardamom Scones

Increase the sugar to $1/2$ cup. Add 1 teaspoon ground cardamom to the flour mixture. Replace the currants with 1 cup chopped almonds. Shape and bake as directed.

Popovers can be baked by themselves at a high temperature, or along with a roast at a lower temperature. Mix the batter up to a day ahead and refrigerate, not only for convenience but also for the highest, lightest popovers. ■ Makes 12 popovers

Popovers

1 cup milk

4 eggs

1 cup all-purpose flour

1 tablespoon sugar

1 teaspoon salt

2 tablespoons butter, melted

1. Mix the milk, eggs, flour, sugar, salt, and butter with a whisk or in a blender, until smooth. Let stand for at least 30 minutes or cover and refrigerate overnight before baking.

2. Position the oven racks so that the top rack is in the center of the oven. If baking along with other food, allow 5 inches between racks for the popovers. Preheat the oven to convection bake at 450°F. Coat two 6-cup ($^1/3$-cup capacity) muffin tins with nonstick spray. Divide the batter among the 12 cups.

3. Bake in the center of the oven for 10 minutes, then reduce the oven temperature to 300°F and bake for 30 more minutes, until the popovers are puffed and golden. Remove from the oven and serve hot.

Note: As an alternative, the popovers can be baked above a roast or chicken with the oven temperature set at 325°F. Bake them on the top rack for an hour, until puffed and crispy.

Pancakes

We used to have oven pancakes (in Finnish, *pannukakku*) every Sunday when the kids were little. With a convection oven they bake in three-quarters of the time and stay puffed longer. I love the toasty, golden edges of the pancake, spread with butter and a bit of jam; suggestions for other toppings are given below.

Brunch Babies *(Pannukakku)*

1^1/3 cups milk

1^1/3 cups eggs (about 6)

1^1/3 cups all-purpose flour

1 tablespoon granulated sugar

1 teaspoon salt

6 tablespoons butter, melted

FOR GARNISH

Powdered sugar

Lemon wedges

Fresh fruit, cut up (bananas, berries, melon)

Whipped cream

These are puffy pancakes baked in 8-inch foil pie tins. Serve one per person. Offer toppings at the table. All six pancakes take just a few minutes to bake to crusty perfection at convection bake. ■ Makes 6 servings

1. Mix the milk, eggs, flour, granulated sugar, and salt with an electric mixer or in a blender, until smooth. Let the batter stand for 30 minutes before baking for best results.

2. Position the oven racks so that they are equally spaced. Preheat the oven to convection bake at 450°F.

3. Brush each of six foil pie tins with 1 tablespoon melted butter. Divide the batter equally among the pie tins, ^{1}/2 cup batter per tin. Place two tins on each oven rack, staggered to allow for air circulation. Bake them for 10 minutes, until puffy and golden.

4. Serve one pancake per person and offer a choice of toppings.

Banana Nut Bread

1 cup coarsely chopped walnuts

1 cup unbleached all-purpose flour

$^1/_2$ cup whole wheat flour

1 cup sugar

1 teaspoon baking powder

$^1/_2$ teaspoon baking soda

$^1/_2$ teaspoon salt

2 eggs

1 cup mashed ripe bananas (about 3 medium)

8 tablespoons (1 stick) butter, melted, or $^1/_2$ cup corn oil or canola oil

1 tablespoon vanilla extract

Whenever bananas get a bit too ripe, I bake banana nut bread and keep a few loaves in the freezer. Whole wheat flour enhances the nuttiness of the loaves. Baking time in the convection oven is reduced by 10 to 15 minutes for either size loaf.

■ Makes one $9^1/_2 \times 5^1/_2$-inch loaf or three $5^3/_4 \times 3^1/_2$-inch loaves

1. Position the oven racks so that they are evenly spaced and one rack is in the center of the oven. Preheat the oven to convection bake at 325°F for a $9^1/_2 \times 5^1/_2$-inch loaf, or 350°F for $5^3/_4 \times 3^1/_2$-inch loaves. Spread the nuts on a baking sheet and toast in the oven as it preheats for 5 to 8 minutes or until fragrant. Cool them. Grease and flour one large or three small loaf pans.

2. Mix the flours, sugar, baking powder, baking soda, and salt in a medium bowl. Add the eggs, bananas, butter, and vanilla and with a hand mixer, beat until the batter is smooth. Stir in the nuts. Pour into one large or three small pans.

3. Bake in the center of the oven for 50 to 55 minutes for the large loaf, 35 to 45 minutes for small loaves, or until a wooden skewer inserted into the center of the loaf comes out clean and dry. Remove the bread from the oven and let it stand in the pan for 5 minutes; loosen the edges with a knife, and turn the bread out of the pan to finish cooling on a wire rack.

Orange Cranberry Bread

1 cup chopped walnuts

2 cups unbleached all-purpose flour

1 cup sugar

1^1/$_2$ teaspoons baking powder

1 teaspoon baking soda

^{1}/$_2$ teaspoon salt

4 tablespoons (^{1}/$_2$ stick) butter, melted

1 egg, beaten

1 teaspoon freshly grated orange zest

Juice from 1 orange plus enough buttermilk
    to make ^{3}/$_4$ cup

1 cup dried cranberries

Dried cranberries, widely available today, fleck the texture of this bread. If you use fresh berries that were frozen, be sure they are at room temperature because frozen berries affect the baking time. Toast the walnuts while preheating the oven.

■ Makes one 9^1/$_2$ × 5^1/$_2$-inch loaf or three 5^3/$_4$ × 3^1/$_2$-inch loaves

1. Position the oven racks so that they are evenly spaced and one rack is in the center of the oven. Preheat the oven to convection bake at 325°F for a 9^1/$_2$ × 5^1/$_2$-inch loaf, or 350°F for 5^3/$_4$ × 3^1/$_2$-inch loaves. Spread the nuts on a baking sheet and toast in the oven as it preheats for 5 to 8 minutes or until fragrant. Cool them. Grease and flour one large or three small loaf pans.

2. In a large mixing bowl, combine the flour, sugar, baking powder, baking soda, and salt. Add the melted butter, egg, orange zest, orange juice and buttermilk mixture, cranberries, and toasted walnuts all at once and stir with a wooden spoon, just until the dry ingredients are moistened.

3. Pour the batter into one large or three small loaf pans. Bake in the center of the oven for 50 to 55 minutes for the large loaf, 35 to 45 minutes for small loaves, or until a wooden skewer inserted into the center of the loaf comes out clean and dry. Remove the bread from the oven and let it stand in the pan for 5 minutes; loosen the edges with a knife, and turn the bread out of the pan to finish cooling on a wire rack.

Blueberry Cream Cheese Coffee Cake

2^1/$_4$ cups unbleached all-purpose flour

1 cup sugar

12 tablespoons (1^1/$_2$ sticks) butter, softened

1^1/$_2$ teaspoons baking powder

^{1}/$_4$ teaspoon salt

^{3}/$_4$ cup sour cream

2 eggs

1 teaspoon almond extract

One 8-ounce package cream cheese, softened

2 cups fresh blueberries

^{1}/$_2$ cup slivered almonds

This will impress your guests when you want something extra special to serve for brunch on a summer morning during blueberry season. I sometimes make an extra cake just for backup and keep it well wrapped in a round metal tin in the freezer. ■ Makes 12 to 16 servings

1. Position the oven racks so that they are evenly spaced and one rack is in the center. Preheat the oven to convection bake at 325°F. Lightly grease the bottom and sides of a 10-inch springform pan and dust with flour.

2. Stir the flour and ^{3}/$_4$ cup of the sugar together in a large bowl. With a pastry blender or a fork, cut in the butter until the mixture resembles coarse crumbs. Reserve 1 cup of the mixture.

3. Add the baking powder, salt, sour cream, 1 egg, and the almond extract to the remaining flour mixture. Mix until a stiff dough forms. Press the dough over the bottom and 2 inches up the sides of the pan; it will be about ^{1}/$_4$ inch thick on the sides.

4. With an electric mixer, beat the cream cheese, the remaining ^{1}/$_4$ cup sugar, and the remaining egg in a small bowl until well blended. Pour the mixture over the dough in the pan and spread evenly. Arrange the blueberries over the top. Mix the almonds with the reserved crumb mixture and sprinkle over the blueberries.

5. Bake in the center of the oven for 35 to 45 minutes or until the filling is set and the crust is golden brown. Cool for 15 minutes, remove the sides of the pan, and finish cooling on a wire rack and transfer to a serving plate.

A ribbon of cinnamon sugar and nuts runs through this coffee cake. This is irresistible served while still warm.

■ Makes 12 servings

Hazelnut Cinnamon Coffee Cake

1 cup hazelnuts or filberts
$1/2$ pound (2 sticks) butter, softened
1 cup granulated sugar
2 eggs
$1^1/2$ cups sour cream
1 teaspoon vanilla extract
2 cups all-purpose flour
$1^1/2$ teaspoons baking powder
$1/2$ teaspoon baking soda
1 tablespoon ground cinnamon
$1/4$ cup packed light brown sugar

1. Position the oven racks so that they are evenly spaced and one rack is in the center. Preheat the oven to convection bake at 325°F. Spread the nuts on a cookie sheet and toast in the oven for 5 to 8 minutes as the oven preheats. Cool and chop. Coat a 10-inch tube pan with nonstick spray and dust with flour.

2. With an electric mixer, cream the butter and granulated sugar together in a large bowl. Add the eggs and beat until light and fluffy. Add the sour cream and vanilla and beat until blended. Mix the flour, baking powder, and baking soda together and add to the egg mixture, beating at low speed until smooth.

3. In a small bowl, stir the chopped nuts, cinnamon, and brown sugar together.

4. Spoon half the batter into the prepared pan. Sprinkle with half the nut mixture. Top with the remaining batter, then with the remaining nut mixture. The top layer of nut mixture will sink into the cake as it bakes.

5. Bake in the center of the oven for 55 to 60 minutes or until a wooden skewer inserted into the center comes out clean and dry. Cool in the pan for 5 minutes. Remove from the pan and place on a serving plate.

Cakes, Cookies, and Desserts

Most cakes include ingredients that make them brown quickly: sugar, shortening, and eggs. This means that the oven temperature must be 25 to 50 degrees lower than in a conventional oven. Use the chart and the recipes in this chapter as guidelines for converting your favorite cake recipes. Whether made from a mix or a favorite recipe, cakes baked in the convection oven retain moisture and flavor and stay fresh longer.

Be sure to check for doneness by inserting a wooden skewer or a toothpick in the center of the cake. If it comes out clean and dry, the cake is done—and that might be a few minutes sooner than you'd expect.

The advantage of baking cookies in the convection oven is that usually you can bake the entire recipe at one time—a great time-saver. Whether made from scratch or a purchased refrigerated dough, cookies need to be baked at a temperature about 25 degrees lower than in the conventional oven. Arrange the oven racks so that they are evenly spaced, with the second rack in the center of the oven. Most ovens come with three racks, although it is possible to purchase a fourth rack.

When I have plans to bake a batch of cookies, I often take out all the ingredients first and then set the oven to preheat. By the time I have the cookie dough mixed and cookies shaped on three pans, the oven is preheated.

For best results, bake cookies on dark, rimless, noninsulated cookie sheets covered with a sheet of parchment paper or a Silpat mat, a nonstick silicone baking pan liner. Silpat mats are expensive, however, and you would need three or more.

When baking purchased frozen pies, follow the directions on the carton but reduce the oven temperature by 25 degrees. Expect the pie to be done in about one-third less time as well.

Guidelines for Baking Cakes in a Convection Oven

The following guidelines will help you to convert your favorite cake recipes to convection baking. You can use the recipes that follow as guidelines, too.

Type of Cake/ Size and Shape of Pan	Convection Bake Temperature	Time	Comments
9 × 13-inch rectangle	325°F or 25 degrees less than favorite recipe, baking time reduced by 5 to 15 minutes	25 to 30 minutes	Use center shelf position or bake several cakes on multiple racks; stagger if possible for best air circulation.
8- or 9-inch square	325°F	30 to 40 minutes	Use center shelf position if baking just one, or bake on multiple levels, staggering pans for best air circulation.
8- or 9-inch round	300°F	30 to 40 minutes	Can bake on multiple levels; stagger pans for best air circulation.
Fluted tube pan	325°F	40 to 45 minutes	Use center shelf position.
Jelly roll pan, any dimension	350°F	9 to 12 minutes	Use center shelf position if baking just one, or bake on multiple levels; same timing.

Type of Cake/ Size and Shape of Pan	Convection Bake Temperature	Time	Comments
Pound cake, loaf	300°F	55 to 65 minutes	Use center shelf position.
Cupcakes	300°F	20 to 25 minutes	Use center shelf position if baking one pan, or bake on multiple levels; same timing.
Angel food	325°F	35 to 45 minutes	Use lower shelf position just below center.
Fruit cake, loaf	275°F	80 to 90 minutes	Use center shelf position if baking just one, or bake, staggered, on multiple levels; same timing.

Use flavorful, tart apples for this cake for the best flavor. Baked on the convection bake mode, it bakes considerably faster than in a conventional oven. ■ Makes 16 servings

Mocha-Flavored Apple Cake

1^1/2 cups all-purpose flour

1 cup sugar

2 teaspoons unsweetened cocoa

1 teaspoon baking soda

1 teaspoon ground cinnamon

^{1}/4 teaspoon salt

^{1}/8 teaspoon ground nutmeg

8 tablespoons (1 stick) butter, softened

2 eggs

2 medium tart cooking apples, peeled, cored, and chopped

1 cup chopped filberts, pecans, or walnuts

^{1}/2 cup cold strong coffee

Maple Caramel Frosting (recipe follows)

1. Position the oven racks so that they are evenly spaced and one rack is in the center. Preheat the oven to convection bake at 325°F. Butter a 9 × 13-inch pan.

2. In a large bowl, combine the flour, sugar, cocoa, baking soda, cinnamon, salt, and nutmeg, and mix well. Add the butter and blend with a hand mixer until the ingredients resemble moist, coarse crumbs.

3. Add the eggs, apples, nuts, and coffee, and mix at low speed for 1 minute. Increase the speed to high and continue mixing until the batter is well blended.

4. Turn the batter into the prepared pan. Bake in the center of the oven for 25 to 30 minutes or until the cake feels firm in the center when touched and a toothpick inserted into the center of the cake comes out clean. Cool the cake on a wire rack. Prepare the frosting and frost the cake when it is cool.

Maple Caramel Frosting

The powdered sugar is measured before sifting. Sifting is needed only if the sugar is lumpy.

■ Makes about 2 cups

4 tablespoons ($^1/_2$ stick) butter
$^1/_2$ cup lightly packed brown sugar
$^1/_4$ cup pure maple syrup
2 tablespoons milk
$^1/_2$ to 1 cup powdered sugar
1 teaspoon vanilla extract

1. Melt the butter in a small saucepan. Add the brown sugar and maple syrup and cook over low heat for 2 minutes.

2. Add the milk and heat to a boil, stirring. Remove the pan from the heat and stir in the powdered sugar and vanilla, mixing until smooth and creamy. If necessary, add a few more drops of milk to get a spreading consistency.

This is just as easy to make as a cake mix, but twice as tasty. ■ Makes 12 to 16 servings

Cocoa Cake with Easy Buttercream Frosting

2 cups all-purpose flour

1^1/3 cups sugar

^{1}/2 cup unsweetened cocoa

1 teaspoon salt

1 tablespoon baking soda

1 cup warm strong coffee

1 cup buttermilk

^{3}/4 cup canola oil or vegetable oil

1 egg

1 tablespoon vanilla extract

Cocoa Buttercream Frosting (recipe follows)

1. Position the oven racks so that they are evenly spaced and one rack is in the center. Preheat the oven to convection bake at 325°F. Butter or grease a 9 × 13-inch cake pan.

2. In a large mixing bowl, stir together the flour, sugar, cocoa, salt, and baking soda until blended. Make an indentation in the center of the dry ingredients and measure in all the remaining ingredients, except the frosting.

3. Mix at low speed with an electric mixer, scraping the sides of the bowl with a spatula, until all

the ingredients are well blended. Turn the mixer speed to high and beat for 2 to 3 minutes, until the batter is smooth and light.

4. Pour the batter into the prepared pan and bake in the center of the oven for 35 to 40 minutes or until a toothpick inserted into the center of the cake comes out clean and dry. Cool the cake on a wire rack. Frost the cake when it is completely cooled.

Cocoa Buttercream Frosting

Melt 8 tablespoons (1 stick) butter in a saucepan. Remove from the heat. Stir in ^{2}/3 cup unsweetened cocoa, 3 cups powdered sugar, ^{1}/3 cup heavy cream, and 1 teaspoon vanilla extract, and continue to stir until the frosting is smooth and creamy.

Strawberry Sponge Layer Cake

1¹/2 cups whole eggs (about 6)

1¹/2 cups granulated sugar

¹/2 teaspoon salt

1¹/2 cups all-purpose flour, stirred before
measuring

2 teaspoons vanilla extract

FOR THE FILLING

¹/4 cup fruit-flavored liqueur such as Cointreau or
Triple Sec, flavored rum, or fruit juice

2 cups sliced fresh strawberries or other berries

2 cups heavy cream, whipped and sweetened with
3 to 4 tablespoons powdered sugar

1. Position the oven racks so that they are evenly spaced and one rack is in the center. Preheat the oven to convection bake at 350°F. Line two 9-inch round cake pans with parchment paper.

2. In the large bowl of an electric mixer, beat the eggs until frothy. Increase the speed and add 1 tablespoon of the granulated sugar and the salt. With the mixer at high speed, add the remaining granulated sugar 1 tablespoon at a time, until the mixture is very light and lemon colored, beating at high speed for at least 5 minutes.

3. Turn the beater to low speed and add half the flour and the vanilla and mix until the flour is evenly blended. Turn off the mixer and add the remaining ³/4 cup of flour. With a rubber spat-

ula, gently blend in the flour until no longer visible.

4. Divide the batter between the two pans. Bake both pans on the center rack of the oven for 20 minutes or until the center of each cake springs back when touched and a toothpick inserted in the center comes out clean and dry. Remove the pans and cool on a wire rack.

5. Loosen the edges of the cake layers from the pans and gently ease the cakes out of the pans. Peel away the parchment.

6. To fill the cake, place one layer on a cake plate and drizzle with 2 tablespoons of the liqueur. Top with half of the fresh berries. Spread half the whipped cream over the berries. Top with the second layer and repeat layering, ending with the remaining whipped cream on top. Refrigerate until ready to serve.

Eggs, sugar, and flour in equal measure are the basis of this simple cake, which bakes in just 20 minutes and can be filled with fruit or berries in season.

■ Makes 12 servings

Lemon Ginger Pound Cake

3 cups all-purpose flour

2 cups sugar

2 teaspoons baking powder

$^1/_2$ teaspoon salt

$^1/_2$ pound (2 sticks) unsalted butter, softened

4 eggs

1 cup milk

Freshly grated zest of 2 lemons

2 teaspoons peeled and grated fresh ginger

FOR THE LEMON GLAZE

$^1/_2$ cup sugar

$^1/_4$ cup freshly squeezed lemon juice

This moist, even-textured cake is wonderful served plain with a cup of herbal tea. When raspberries are in season, top slices with the berries. To gild the lily, add a dollop of whipped cream.

■ Makes four $7^1/_2$ x $3^1/_2$-inch loaves
or two 9 x 5 x 3-inch loaves

1. Position the oven racks so that they are evenly spaced and one rack is in the center. Preheat the oven to convection bake at 325°F. Butter and flour four $7^1/_2$ x $3^1/_2$-inch loaf pans or two 9 x 5 x 3-inch loaf pans.

2. In the large bowl of an electric mixer, combine the flour, sugar, baking powder, and salt. Cut the butter into small pieces and add to the dry ingredients; mix until the butter is thoroughly incorporated into the dry ingredients.

3. Add the eggs, milk, lemon zest, and ginger, and beat at low speed for about 2 minutes, until blended. Scrape the sides of the bowl with a rubber spatula and beat for 3 to 5 more minutes, until the batter is light and fluffy.

4. Turn the batter into the prepared pans. Place the pans in the center of the oven and bake the small loaves for 25 to 30 minutes, the large loaves for 55 to 65 minutes, or until a toothpick inserted into the center of a cake comes out clean and dry.

5. While the cakes bake, make the lemon glaze by mixing together the sugar and lemon juice. Brush the tops of the hot cakes with the glaze. Remove the cakes from the pans and cool on a wire rack.

Orange Walnut Cake

2^1/$_2$ cups all-purpose flour

1 cup sugar

2 tablespoons freshly grated orange zest (about
   2 oranges)

1 teaspoon baking soda

1 teaspoon baking powder

^{1}/$_2$ pound (2 sticks) butter, softened

2 eggs, at room temperature

1 cup buttermilk

^{1}/$_2$ cup chopped walnuts

FOR THE ORANGE SYRUP

1 cup freshly squeezed orange juice

1 cup sugar

This old-fashioned cake is bathed in an orange syrup when it is still hot from the oven. ■ Makes 12 to 16 servings

1. Position the oven racks so that the top rack is in the center. Preheat the oven to convection bake at 325°F. Lightly grease a 9-inch tube pan.

2. In a large bowl, mix the flour, sugar, orange zest, baking soda, and baking powder together. Add the butter, eggs, and buttermilk all at once and, using a hand mixer, beat until the mixture is smooth. Stir in the walnuts.

3. Pour the batter into the prepared pan and smooth the batter to the edges. Bake for 40 to 45 minutes or until a toothpick inserted into the center of the cake comes out clean and dry. Remove from the oven, leaving the cake in the pan.

4. While the cake bakes, make the orange syrup by combining the orange juice and sugar; bring to a boil and stir until the sugar is dissolved.

5. Poke the hot cake with a skewer in several places and pour the hot syrup over it. Cool the cake on a wire rack for at least 15 minutes before removing it from the pan to a serving plate.

This popular dessert can be made a day ahead and baked at the last minute. The chile powder adds a mild heat and enhances the chocolate flavor. ■ Makes six 4-ounce desserts

Melted-Center Ancho Chocolate Cakes

Butter and sugar for the baking dishes

8 tablespoons (1 stick) butter

Six 1-ounce squares bittersweet or semisweet
    chocolate

2 tablespoons all-purpose flour

$1/2$ teaspoon ancho chile powder

1 teaspoon vanilla extract

3 eggs

$1/4$ cup granulated sugar

Powdered sugar and berries for garnish

1. Position the oven racks so that they are evenly spaced and one rack is in the center. Preheat the oven to convection bake at 400°F. Butter and lightly sugar six 4-ounce ramekins, custard cups, or baking cups and tap out the excess sugar. Set on a baking sheet.

2. Melt the butter and chocolate together in a small, heavy saucepan over low heat. Remove from the heat. Stir in the flour, ancho powder, and vanilla. Set aside.

3. In the bowl of an electric mixer, beat the eggs and granulated sugar at high speed until thick

and lemon colored, scraping the sides of the bowl often, about 5 minutes.

4. Mix the chocolate quickly into the egg mixture.

5. Spoon the mixture into the prepared baking cups and bake for 8 minutes for glass custard cups, 10 minutes for porcelain ramekins, or until the sides of the cakes are firm but the centers are still soft (they will jiggle slightly).

6. Remove the cakes from the oven and let them cool in the baking dishes for 3 minutes. Loosen the edges with a butter knife. Place a dessert plate on top of each and invert onto the plate. Let stand for 1 minute and remove the baking cup.

7. Dust with powdered sugar and garnish with a fresh strawberry or raspberry before serving.

Notes: To reduce the sweetness, use 3 ounces unsweetened chocolate and 3 ounces bitter-sweet chocolate. Ancho chile powder is available in specialty food stores featuring Southwestern and Mexican foods.

Chocolate Soufflé

1/4 cup cornstarch

1 1/4 cups light cream or milk

3/4 cup granulated sugar

2 tablespoons butter

4 ounces semisweet chocolate, melted

4 eggs, separated

2 egg whites

1/8 teaspoon salt

1 teaspoon cream of tartar

1 cup heavy cream

2 tablespoons powdered sugar

1. Position the oven racks so that the top rack is one level below the center of the oven. Preheat the oven to convection bake at 350°F. Lightly butter and dust with sugar a 2 1/2-quart soufflé dish. Cut a 12-inch-wide sheet of foil so it is 4 inches longer than the circumference of the soufflé dish. Fold it into thirds lengthwise, butter it, and sugar it lightly. Place the buttered side of the foil around the dish so that it extends 2 1/2 inches above the rim. Fold the ends to seal securely.

2. Mix the cornstarch with half of the cream in a saucepan, then mix in the remaining cream and 1/2 cup of the granulated sugar. Bring to a boil, stirring constantly, and cook until thickened and smooth. Dot with the butter. Blend in the melted chocolate. Cool for 5 minutes and whisk in the egg yolks.

3. Whip the 6 egg whites until foamy. Add the salt and cream of tartar and beat in the remaining 1/4 cup granulated sugar. Whip until the whites form stiff peaks.

4. Fold one-quarter of the egg whites into the chocolate sauce, then fold in the remaining whites gently so they do not deflate. Pour the batter into the prepared dish. Bake for 25 minutes for a saucy center, or just until the soufflé slightly "ripples" in the center when shaken. Bake for 30 to 35 minutes for a soufflé that is evenly set. Serve immediately.

5. While the soufflé bakes, whip the cream and sweeten with the powdered sugar. Serve in a bowl.

To synchronize a dessert soufflé with the rest of the meal, you can get the whole thing ready for baking an hour ahead, and pop it into the oven about 25 minutes before you plan to serve dessert. ■ Makes 6 servings

Apple Kuchen

12 tablespoons (1^1/2 sticks) butter, softened

^{3}/4 cup granulated sugar, plus 2 tablespoons

3 eggs

1 teaspoon vanilla extract

1^1/2 cups all-purpose flour

^{1}/2 teaspoon baking powder

^{1}/2 teaspoon salt

5 small apples, such as McIntosh, Cortland, Granny
    Smith, or Golden Delicious, peeled, cored, and
    cut into 8 wedges

2 tablespoons butter, melted

Powdered sugar

As if by magic, this cake creates its own beautiful picture as it bakes. Spread a buttery dough onto a shallow pan and press apple wedges into the top; as the kuchen bakes the dough rises up to frame the apples. This is delicious served warm from the oven topped with a scoop of vanilla ice cream.

■ Makes about 12 servings

1. Position the oven racks so that they are evenly spaced, with one rack in the center of the oven. Preheat the oven to convection bake at 400°F. Butter a 12-inch tart pan or a 9 × 13-inch cake pan.

2. Cream the softened butter and ^{3}/4 cup of the granualted sugar until light in a large bowl, using an electric mixer; add the eggs and vanilla and beat until light and fluffy. Add the flour, baking powder, and salt to make a smooth dough.

3. Spread the dough into the prepared pan.

4. With a sharp knife, make lengthwise cuts in the apples, ^{1}/4 inch apart but not all the way through, so the halves still hold together. Press the apple wedges, cut side down, evenly into the batter. Brush the apples with the melted butter and sprinkle with the remaining 2 tablespoons granulated sugar.

5. Bake on the center rack for 25 minutes, until the cake is golden and the apples are cooked through. Remove from the oven and cool on a wire rack. Sprinkle with powdered sugar.

Old-Fashioned Jelly Roll

3 eggs, at room temperature

1 cup granulated sugar

1 teaspoon vanilla extract

1 cup all-purpose flour

2 teaspoons baking powder

$1/2$ teaspoon salt

$1/3$ cup powdered sugar, plus more for garnish

Whipped cream for garnish

FOR THE FILLING

1 cup fruit jelly, 1 cup chocolate ganache, or 2 cups
    whipped cream and 1 pint berries

This is a basic recipe for a simple-to-make jelly roll. Instead of spreading the cake with jelly, you can spread it with whipped cream and sprinkle with fresh berries before you roll up the cake. Another option is to substitute a rich chocolate ganache and roll up the cake before the ganache sets. ■ Makes 8 servings

1. Position the oven racks so that they are evenly spaced, with one rack in the center of the oven. Preheat the oven to convection bake at 350°F. Line a 15 × 10-inch jelly roll pan with parchment paper and coat the parchment with nonstick spray.

2. In a large bowl, beat the eggs with an electric mixer on the highest speed for about 3 minutes, until foamy. Add the granulated sugar, 1 table-spoon at a time, beating until very light and fluffy. By hand, stir in $1/4$ cup cold water and the vanilla. Fold in the flour, baking powder, and salt, and blend well.

3. Pour the batter into the prepared pan and smooth it out. Bake in the center of the oven for 9 to 12 minutes, until the top feels dry when touched.

4. While the cake bakes, sprinkle the powdered sugar over a clean tea towel or a long strip of paper towel. Loosen the sides of the cake from the pan and invert it onto the towel. Remove the parchment paper and roll the cake up, starting at a narrow end, allowing the towel to be rolled up inside. Place it on a rack to cool. When cool, unroll the cake, spread it with your choice of filling, and roll it up again.

5. Dust the roll with additional powdered sugar or spread with whipped cream. Cut into cross-wise slices to serve.

Long, slow baking in the convection oven produces a beautiful cake, one that has a silky texture. A bit of flour in the mixture makes the cake easier to cut. This makes a large cheesecake, ideal for a party. Top it with fresh berries in season or use one of the variations below.

■ Makes 16 servings

The Ultimate Cheesecake

1 cup zwieback crumbs

$^1/_4$ cup packed brown sugar

2 tablespoons butter, melted

Five 8-ounce packages ($2^1/_2$ pounds) cream
   cheese, softened

$1^2/_3$ cups sugar

3 tablespoons all-purpose flour

1 teaspoon freshly grated lemon zest, or
   $^1/_4$ teaspoon pure lemon oil

1 teaspoon freshly grated orange zest, or
   $^1/_4$ teaspoon pure orange oil

1 teaspoon vanilla extract

$^1/_4$ teaspoon salt

6 eggs, at room temperature

$^1/_4$ cup sour cream

Optional topping (see recipes below)

1. Position the oven racks so that they are evenly spaced, with one rack in the center of the oven. Preheat the oven to convection bake at 350°F. Generously butter the bottom and sides of a 10-inch springform pan.

2. Stir together the zwieback crumbs, brown sugar, and melted butter in a small bowl. Press the crumb mixture evenly into the bottom of the buttered pan. Bake for 10 minutes, until the crust is lightly browned. Remove from the oven and reduce the oven temperature to convection bake at 300°F.

3. Beat the cream cheese in the bowl of an electric mixer until light and fluffy. Combine the sugar and flour in a separate bowl. Stir into the cream cheese along with the lemon zest, orange zest, vanilla, salt, eggs, and sour cream. Beat at low speed, scraping the bowl often, until well blended.

4. Pour the batter into the pan and bake in the center of the oven for an hour, until set but still slightly jiggly. Turn the oven off, open the oven door, and allow the cake to cool in the oven for 10 minutes. Chill several hours or overnight. Serve plain or decorate as described below.

Sour Cream–Rum Topping

Mix 2 cups sour cream, 2 tablespoons sugar, and 1 tablespoon dark rum or bourbon until smooth. Spread on top of the cheesecake after the cake has baked for $1^1/2$ hours and return it to the oven for 5 minutes before cooling.

Chocolate Turtle Topping

Drizzle the top of chilled cake with $^1/2$ cup toasted pecans and 3 to 4 tablespoons caramel ice cream topping and 3 to 4 tablespoons chocolate ice cream topping.

Guidelines for Baking Cookies and Bars in a Convection Oven

The following guidelines will help you to convert your favorite cookie and bar recipes to convection baking. Baking times are only slightly reduced. If you find that your cookies are baking unevenly, reduce the oven temperature by 25 degrees: ovens vary. You can use the recipes that follow as guidelines, too.

Type of Cookie/ Bar Size and Shape of Pan	Convection Bake Temperature	Time	Comments
Drop and shaped cookies, e.g., peanut butter, chocolate chip, spritz, molded butter cookies	350°F	0 to 12 minutes, single- or multiple-rack baking	The sweeter the cookie, the more quickly it bakes. If cookies on multiple racks brown unevenly, lower the oven temperature by 25 degrees. Baking time may increase 1 to 2 minutes.
Rolled, cut-out cookies	350°F	5 to 8 minutes, single- or multiple-rack baking	Thin cookies bake in less time than thick; watch carefully. If cookies on multiple racks brown unevenly, lower the oven temperature by 25 degrees. Baking time may increase 1 to 2 minutes.
Brownies from mix or scratch; 9 × 13-inch pan	325°F	22 to 25 minutes	Bake until toothpick inserted 2 inches from side of pan comes out almost clean; cool. Overbaked brownies will be dry.
Brownies from mix or scratch; 9 × 9-inch pan	325°F	33 to 35 minutes	Bake until toothpick inserted 2 inches from side of pan comes out almost clean; cool.

Type of Cookie/ Bar Size and Shape of Pan	Convection Bake Temperature	Time	Comments
Bars with prebaked crust, with filling and topping	325°F or 25 degrees less than favorite recipe	Baking time slightly reduced	Bars in this category: lemon bars, apple-filled bars, toffee bars, date-filled bars with oatmeal crust.
Biscotti (twice-baked cookies)	325°F (or 25 degrees less than favorite recipe), plus 275°F for second bake	Biscotti can be baked on multiple racks in the oven	If cookies on multiple racks brown unevenly, lower the oven temperature by 25 degrees. Baking time may increase 3 to 4 minutes (see recipe).
Meringue-based cookies, e.g., meringue kisses	175° to 200°F or 25 degrees less than favorite recipe	1 to 1^1/2 hours	Meringues need to dry in the oven rather than bake to achieve a dry/crisp exterior and interior. If baked at too high a temperature the center is chewy, the exterior browned; bake on parchment paper for best results.
Madeleines, sandbakkels, or cookies baked in metal molds	400°F or 25 degrees less than favorite recipe	Baking time shortened by 5 minutes	Baking time varies a little with the ingredient mix; sugar affects baking time and crispness of the final product; if cookie is high in sugar, baking time is shorter.

Tips

- For the best results, bake cookies on dark, rimless, noninsulated cookie sheets. If you use cookie sheets with rims, the cookies will not bake evenly. Select heavy-gauge baking sheets to keep cookies from "warping" while baking.

- Use parchment paper or Silpats to line cookie sheets and prevent cookies from sticking while baking. Parchment paper also allows cookies to brown evenly on top and bottom. With parchment paper, you can simply slide cookies, paper and all, onto a countertop to cool. A cooling rack is not necessary.

- Cookies bake evenly on multiple racks at the same time, in most convection ovens. If you have trouble with uneven baking, lower the baking temperature by 25 degrees and bake a minute or two longer.

- For more delicate cookies, such as sugar cookies or basic butter cookies, use unsalted butter; otherwise, for most drop cookies lightly salted butter is fine.

Sugar Cookies

1/2 pound (2 sticks) unsalted butter, softened

1 cup sugar

2 eggs

3 cups all-purpose flour

1 teaspoon baking soda

1/8 teaspoon salt

Colored sugar or thin icing for decoration, optional

This is the simplest of doughs for cut-out cookies, but the best! Bake three sheets of cookies at a time and reduce the oven temperature to 300°F for the most even baking.

■ Makes 5 to 6 dozen cookies

1. In the large bowl of an electric mixer, cream the butter and sugar. Add the eggs and blend until smooth. In a separate bowl, stir the flour, baking soda, and salt together and add to the creamed mixture, mixing at low speed until the dough is smooth. Shape the dough into a ball, wrap the dough in plastic, and refrigerate for at least 2 hours, or up to 4 days.

2. Position the oven racks so that they are evenly spaced. Preheat the oven to convection bake at 300°F. Cover three dark, rimless, non-insulated cookie sheets with parchment paper.

3. Remove the dough from the refrigerator and cut it into quarters. Roll out one part of the dough at a time on a floured board. Cut out cookies using your favorite cookie cutters and place them on the prepared cookie sheets. If desired, sprinkle the cookies with colored sugar or decorations, or decorate with thin icing after they have cooled.

4. Bake on multiple racks for 10 minutes, until very lightly browned around the edges. Remove from the oven and slide cookies and parchment onto the counter to cool.

Brown sugar in these cut-out cookies gives them a rich, caramel-butterscotch flavor. Use any cookie cutters, or follow the directions for Praline-Filled Chocolate Drizzle Cookies (page 217) for delicious cookies shaped, filled, and frosted in mass-production style. ■ Makes 5 to 6 dozen cookies

Brown Sugar Cookies

$1/2$ pound (2 sticks) unsalted butter, softened

$1/2$ cup packed dark or light brown sugar

$1/2$ cup granulated sugar

1 teaspoon vanilla extract

2 eggs

3 cups all-purpose flour

1 teaspoon baking soda

$1/4$ teaspoon salt

1. In the large bowl of an electric mixer, cream the butter and sugars. Add the vanilla and eggs and beat until light and fluffy. In a separate bowl, stir the flour, baking soda, and salt together and add it to the creamed mixture; mix on low speed until smooth. Shape the dough into a ball, wrap it in plastic, and chill for 1 hour or refrigerate for up to 4 days.

2. Position the oven racks so that they are evenly spaced. Preheat the oven to convection bake at 350°F. Cover three dark, rimless, noninsulated cookie sheets with parchment paper.

3. Remove the dough from the refrigerator and cut it into quarters. Roll out one part of the dough at a time on a floured board. Cut out cookies using your favorite cookie cutters and place them on the prepared cookie sheets.

4. Bake on multiple racks for 10 minutes, until very lightly browned around the edges. Cool on wire racks.

Praline-Filled Chocolate Drizzle Cookies

FOR THE PRALINE FILLING

$^1/_2$ cup heavy cream

$^1/_2$ cup packed dark or light brown sugar

$^1/_2$ cup chopped pecans

FOR THE CHOCOLATE DRIZZLE ICING

$^1/_2$ cup (2 ounces) semisweet chocolate chips

$^1/_2$ cup (2 ounces) chopped pure white chocolate

Brown Sugar Cookie dough (page 216), refrigerated

1. To make the praline filling, combine the cream, brown sugar, and pecans in a saucepan. Bring to a boil over medium-high heat. Boil for 2 to 3 minutes, stirring, until thick. Remove from the heat and cool.

2. To make the chocolate icing, place the chocolate chips into a pint-sized, heavy zip-top plastic bag. Place the white chocolate into another pint-sized, heavy zip-top plastic bag. Close both bags securely and place in a large bowl of very hot water. Let them stand until the chocolates are melted.

3. To shape and bake the cookies, position the oven racks so that they are evenly spaced. Preheat the oven to convection bake at 325°F. Have three ungreased dark, rimless, noninsulated cookie sheets ready.

4. Divide the refrigerated dough into 6 equal parts. Shape each piece into a smooth log about 12 inches long. Place the logs lengthwise on three separate dark, rimless, noninsulated cookie sheets, two on each pan, and flatten with your palm. With a rolling pin, roll out the dough to the length of the cookie sheet and about 3 inches wide, with a 3-inch space between each of the strips of dough. Trim the ends and sides to make straight-sided rectangles.

5. With a straight-edged knife, score the dough into $1^1/_2$-inch squares. Drop about $^1/_2$ teaspoon of the praline filling into the center of each square. Bake on multiple racks for 7 to 9 minutes or until golden on the edges. Remove the cookies from the oven and, while still warm, separate them along the score marks using a straight-edged knife.

6. Cut a small triangle across one corner of each bag of melted chocolate. Squeeze to decoratively drizzle chocolate over the cookies. Leave the cookies on the cookie sheet and cool until the chocolate is set.

These are my favorite "mass-production" cookies. So, when I have little time to bake, these are the cookies I choose.

■ Makes 5 to 6 dozen cookies

Buttery and delicious, this dough can be flavored and shaped many different ways. In the convection oven I bake three pans at a time. For the best flavor, wrap and refrigerate the dough for at least 24 hours. During this time the butter and additional flavors (see variations) develop.

■ Makes 4 to 5 dozen cookies

Butter Cookies (Basic Dough)

$^1/_2$ pound (2 sticks) unsalted butter, softened
$^1/_2$ cup powdered sugar
1 egg yolk
1 teaspoon vanilla extract
$^1/_4$ teaspoon salt
3$^1/_2$ cups all-purpose flour

1. Measure all the ingredients into the large bowl of an electric mixer. Turn the mixer on low and mix until a dough forms, scraping the sides of the bowl. Wrap the dough in plastic and refrigerate for at least 24 hours or up to 2 days.

2. Position the oven racks so that they are evenly spaced. Preheat the oven to convection bake at 350°F. Cover three dark, rimless, noninsulated cookie sheets with parchment paper.

3. Shape the cookies and bake all three pans at the same time as directed in the following variations.

Raspberry Ribbons

Divide the dough into 6 parts. On a lightly floured surface, with your palms, roll each part out to make a strand about $^3/4$ inch in diameter and the length of the cookie sheet.

Place the strands, well separated, on the

cookie sheets, two to a sheet. With the side of your little finger press a groove down the length of each strand. Bake for 8 minutes or until the cookies feel firm to the touch.

Remove from the oven and spoon about 1 tablespoon raspberry jam into the groove for the full length of each partially baked strand. Return to the oven for 5 to 8 minutes or until the cookies are lightly browned on the edges.

Meanwhile, mix $1/2$ cup powdered sugar, 2 teaspoons freshly squeezed lemon juice, and 1 teaspoon cream or water to make a thin icing. Drizzle the icing down the length of the hot cookies. Cut the strands into 1- or $1^1/2$-inch lengths. Let them cool on the parchment paper on the counter.

Candy Cane Cookies

Divide the dough into 2 pieces. Flavor one piece with 5 to 6 drops anise or peppermint extract and add a few drops of red food coloring, mixing it in evenly. Refrigerate both pieces as directed in the basic recipe.

Working with a small amount at a time from each batch, roll the dough into $1/4$-inch-wide strips, trimming to even the edges. Cut the strips into 3-inch lengths and twist a red strand and a white strand together to make each cookie. Curve one end to shape into candy canes; place them on the prepared cookie sheets.

Bake on multiple racks for 5 to 8 minutes or until the cookies are firm and just barely browned on the edges. Cool on the parchment paper on the counter.

Maple Hazelnut Crescents

Make the Butter Cookie dough, using $1/3$ cup packed light or dark brown sugar for the powdered sugar and add $1/2$ teaspoon maple flavoring and 1 cup finely chopped, toasted filberts or hazelnuts. Refrigerate as directed.

Remove the dough from the refrigerator and cut it into 4 pieces. Shape each into a long log and cut each log into 16 pieces. Roll each piece between your palms to make a short log about $1^1/2$ inches long and tapered on each end. Place the cookies 2 inches apart on the prepared baking sheets and shape into crescents.

Bake the cookies on multiple racks for 9 to 11 minutes, until they feel firm and are very lightly browned. Dust heavily with powdered sugar and cool on the parchment paper on the counter completely before storing in an airtight container.

Lemon Sugar Cookies

1/2 pound (2 sticks) unsalted butter, softened

1/2 cup powdered sugar

1/2 cup granulated sugar, plus 1/3 cup for rolling
the cookies

1 teaspoon vanilla extract

1 egg

Freshly grated zest of 1 lemon (about 2 teaspoons)

1 tablespoon freshly squeezed lemon juice

2 cups all-purpose flour

1/2 teaspoon baking soda

1/4 teaspoon salt

These are shaped rather than rolled cookies. To shape even-sized cookies it is helpful to use a #40 ice cream scoop that measures exactly 1 tablespoon of dough. Arrange the oven racks so they are evenly spaced. This works best for most cookies and multiple pans will bake evenly at the same time. ■ Makes 3 1/2 dozen cookies

1. Measure all the ingredients except for the 1/3 cup granulated sugar into the large bowl of an electric mixer. Turn the mixer on low and mix until a dough forms, scraping the bowl's sides.

2. Cover the dough and refrigerate for 2 hours or until just firm. If you chill the dough until it is hard, remove it from the refrigerator about 1 hour before shaping so it can soften enough to be pliable.

3. Position the oven racks so that they are evenly spaced. Preheat the oven to convection bake at 350°F. Cover three dark, rimless, nonin-sulated cookie sheets with parchment paper or use ungreased cookie sheets. Scoop out table-spoon-sized portions of the dough and shape into balls. Roll them in additional granulated sugar and place on the cookie sheets, evenly spaced.

4. Bake the cookies on multiple racks for 9 to 10 minutes, until lightly browned around the edges. Remove from the oven and slide the cookies with the parchment onto a countertop to cool, or remove them from the ungreased cookie sheets to a wire rack to cool.

Cardamom-Ginger Sugar Cookies

Replace the lemon zest with 2 teaspoons peeled and grated fresh ginger and add 1 teaspoon freshly ground cardamom to the creamed mix-ture. Mix and bake as directed.

Chocolate Chip Cookies

2 cups unbleached all-purpose flour
$^1/_2$ teaspoon baking powder
$^1/_2$ teaspoon baking soda
$^1/_4$ teaspoon salt
$^3/_4$ cup granulated sugar
$^1/_2$ cup packed brown sugar
$^1/_2$ pound (2 sticks) butter, softened
2 eggs
1 tablespoon vanilla extract
1 cup semisweet chocolate chips
1 cup coarsely chopped walnuts

1. Position the oven racks so that they are evenly spaced. Preheat the oven to convection bake at 350°F. Cover three dark, rimless, noninsulated cookie sheets with parchment paper or lightly grease them.

2. Measure all the ingredients into the large bowl of an electric mixer. Turn the mixer on low and mix until a dough forms, scraping the sides of the bowl.

3. Using a small ice cream scoop, shape the dough into 48 balls, arrange 16 balls on each prepared cookie sheet, and flatten them slightly.

Chocolate chip cookies are by far the most popular home-baked variety. Using the convection bake mode you can bake multiple sheets of cookies at one time. Just be sure to use dark, rimless, noninsulated cookie sheets. If you use cookie sheets with rims, the cookies will not bake evenly. I also prefer to cover the cookie sheets with parchment paper or Silpats.

■ Makes about 4 dozen cookies

4. Bake the cookies on multiple racks for 8 to 11 minutes, until lightly browned. Remove from the oven and slide the cookies with the parchment onto a countertop to cool, or remove them from the greased cookie sheets to a wire rack to cool.

White Chocolate Chip Macadamia Cookies

Use white chocolate chips for the chocolate and coarsely chopped macadamia nuts for the walnuts.

Oatmeal Nut Cookies

Chewy with nuts, coconut, dried fruit, and chocolate chips. Using my quick one-bowl method, you can stir up the cookie dough in the same time it takes for the oven to preheat.

■ Makes 3 dozen cookies

$^1/_2$ cup packed light or dark brown sugar

$^1/_4$ cup granulated sugar

$^1/_2$ cup unbleached all-purpose flour

$^1/_2$ teaspoon baking soda

$^1/_4$ teaspoon salt

$1^1/_2$ cups rolled oats

$^1/_2$ cup chopped pecans or walnuts

$^1/_2$ cup shredded coconut

$^1/_2$ cup semisweet chocolate chips

$^1/_2$ cup raisins or dried cranberries

1 teaspoon vanilla extract

1 egg

8 tablespoons (1 stick) butter, softened

1. Position the oven racks so that they are evenly spaced. Preheat the oven to convection bake at 350°F. Cover three rimless cookie sheets with parchment paper or lightly grease them.

2. Measure all the ingredients into the large bowl of an electric mixer. Turn the mixer on low and mix until a dough forms, scraping the sides of the bowl.

3. Using a small ice cream scoop, shape the dough into balls, arrange them on the prepared cookie sheets, and flatten them slightly.

4. Bake the cookies on multiple racks for 8 to 10 minutes, until evenly browned. Remove from the oven and slide the cookies with the parchment onto a countertop to cool, or remove them from the greased cookie sheets to a wire rack to cool.

Peanut Butter Cookies

12 tablespoons (1^1/2 sticks) butter, softened
^{3}/4 cup peanut butter, creamy or chunk style
^{1}/2 cup packed light or dark brown sugar
^{1}/4 cup granulated sugar
1 egg
2 cups unbleached all-purpose flour
^{3}/4 teaspoon baking powder
^{3}/4 teaspoon baking soda
^{1}/4 teaspoon salt

1. Position the oven racks so that they are evenly spaced. Preheat the oven to convection bake at 350°F. Cover three rimless noninsulated cookie sheets with parchment paper.

2. Measure all the ingredients into the large bowl of an electric mixer. Turn the mixer on low and mix until a dough forms, scraping the sides of the bowl.

3. Scoop the dough into balls the size of large walnuts and place them about 3 inches apart on the prepared cookie sheets, 12 cookies to a sheet. With a fork dipped in flour, flatten the balls, making a crisscross pattern on each cookie.

4. Bake on multiple racks for 10 to 12 minutes or until the cookies are set. Slide the cookies with the parchment onto a countertop to cool.

These cookies are a little less sweet than most. Preheat the convection oven while you quickly mix up the dough. Space the oven racks evenly in the oven and bake three panfuls at one time.

■ Makes 3 dozen cookies

In the convection oven, the baking temperature is reduced from 375°F to 350°F, and the baking time from 12 to 9 minutes. If that alone isn't enough to convince you to turn on the convection bake mode, I bake three sheets of cookies at one time, which is what the recipe yields, reducing the total baking time from 36 to 9 minutes. ■ Makes 4 dozen cookies

Molasses Spice Cookies

8 tablespoons (1 stick) butter, softened
$1/4$ cup vegetable shortening
1 cup packed brown sugar
1 egg
$1/4$ cup dark molasses
$2 1/4$ cups all-purpose flour
1 teaspoon baking soda
$1 1/2$ teaspoons ground cinnamon
1 teaspoon ground ginger
$1/2$ teaspoon ground cloves
$1/3$ cup granulated sugar

1. Position the oven racks so that they are evenly spaced. Preheat the oven to convection bake at 350°F. Cover three cookie sheets with parchment paper.

2. Measure all the ingredients except for the $1/3$ cup granulated sugar into the large bowl of an electric mixer. Turn the mixer on low and mix until a dough forms, scraping the sides of the bowl.

3. Shape the dough into balls the size of walnuts. Roll them in the granulated sugar and place them 2 inches apart on the prepared cookie sheets, dividing the cookies evenly between the three sheets. Bake on multiple racks for 8 to 9 minutes or until lightly browned. Do not overbake. Slide the cookies with the parchment onto a countertop to cool.

Fudgy Walnut Brownies

2 ounces unsweetened chocolate (2 squares)

8 tablespoons (1 stick) unsalted butter

2 eggs

1 cup sugar

1 teaspoon vanilla extract

$^1/_4$ teaspoon salt

$^1/_2$ cup all-purpose flour

$^1/_2$ cup chopped walnuts

1. Position the oven racks so that one rack is in the center of the oven. Preheat the oven to convection bake at 325°F. Butter an 8-inch square pan.

2. Place the chocolate and butter together in a small, heavy saucepan over the lowest heat and stir until melted together.

3. With an electric mixer, beat the eggs, sugar, vanilla, and salt on low speed in a mixing bowl until light. Add the chocolate and butter mixture. Stir in the flour and walnuts. Pour the batter into the baking pan.

4. Bake on the center rack for 20 to 25 minutes, until the brownies are just barely set. Remove from the oven and cool completely before cutting.

These brownies turn out moist and fudgy. They bake in the convection oven at 25 degrees lower and for 10 minutes less baking time. ■ Makes 12 squares

Chocolate Almond Biscotti

2 cups all-purpose flour

$^1/_3$ cup unsweetened cocoa

1 teaspoon baking powder

$^1/_2$ teaspoon baking soda

$^1/_4$ teaspoon salt

4 ounces semisweet or bittersweet chocolate,
    coarsely chopped

3 eggs, at room temperature

1 cup sugar

2 teaspoons vanilla extract

$^1/_2$ teaspoon almond extract

$1^1/_2$ cups almonds, skins on and lightly toasted

1. Position the oven racks so that they are evenly spaced, with one rack in the center. Preheat the oven to convection bake at 325°F. Line a cookie sheet with parchment paper.

2. In a medium bowl, mix together the flour, cocoa, baking powder, baking soda, and salt. Put the chocolate and $^1/_2$ cup of the flour mixture in the bowl of a food processor fitted with the steel blade. Process for 1 minute, until the chocolate is very finely ground. Remove from the processor and mix with the remaining flour mixture.

3. In the bowl of an electric mixer, beat the eggs and sugar together at high speed until pale and thick. Beat in the vanilla and almond extract. Reduce the speed and gradually mix in the flour and chocolate mixture. Turn off the mixer and stir in the almonds.

4. Divide the dough in half. Shape each part into a log 12 to 14 inches long and 2 inches wide and place on the prepared cookie sheet, spacing the logs at least 4 inches apart. Bake in the center of the oven for 20 to 25 minutes, until firm to the touch.

5. Remove the cookie sheet from the oven and place it on a wire rack to cool for 10 minutes. Reduce the oven temperature to 275°F.

6. Slide the baked logs onto a cutting board. Using a long serrated knife, cut each log diagonally into $1/2$-inch slices. Arrange the biscotti cut side down on two or three cookie sheets lined with parchment paper. Place them in the oven on multiple racks and bake for 7 to 8 minutes on one side, turning the cookies over to bake for 7 to 8 more minutes. Remove the biscotti to a wire rack and let cool completely. Store them at room temperature in an airtight container for about a month, or freeze them for up to 5 months.

You can use these directions to adapt your favorite biscotti recipe to bake in the convection oven. Both temperature and baking time are reduced, plus you can bake on multiple racks with even results.

■ Makes 4 dozen biscotti

Guidelines for Baking Dessert Pies in a Convection Oven

In general, the baking temperature is reduced by 25 degrees and the baking time by one-quarter to one-third.

Type of Pie	Convection Bake Temperature	Time	Comments
Fruit pie, fresh, double crust	400°F	40 to 45 minutes	For a single pie, place in the center of the oven. If baking three or more at one time, stagger among evenly spaced oven racks.
Fruit pie, frozen, double crust	400°F	35 to 45 minutes	See comments above.
Fruit pie, lattice crust	375°F	35 to 45 minutes	See comments above.
Fruit pie, streusel crust	375°F	35 to 45 minutes	See comments above.
Pumpkin pie, homemade	350°F	35 to 45 minutes	See comments above.
Pumpkin pie, frozen	350°F	35 to 45 minutes	See comments above.
Pecan pie, homemade	350°F	35 to 45 minutes	See comments above.
Pecan pie, frozen	350°F	35 to 45 minutes	See comments above.
Lemon meringue pie, meringue bake	400°F	4 to 5 minutes	If meringue browns too quickly, reduce temperature by 25 degrees.
Pastry shell	425°F	7 to 11 minutes	For a single crust partially prebaked, weight down with pie weights or uncooked dried beans.

An apple pie "made from scratch" has no competition from store-bought pies. Here's the basic recipe with some favorite variations. To bake a frozen apple pie, see the chart. Convection-baked pies cook in about one-third less time. ■ Makes one 9-inch pie

Apple Pie

Flaky Pastry (page 37)
About 6 medium tart apples, pared, cored, and
    thinly sliced (6 cups)
$^3/_4$ cup sugar
3 tablespoons all-purpose flour
$1^1/_2$ teaspoons ground cinnamon
$^1/_2$ teaspoon ground nutmeg, optional
$^1/_4$ teaspoon kosher salt
2 tablespoons butter, cut up
Milk for brushing the top of the pie
Sugar or cinnamon sugar for the top of the pie,
    optional

1. Position the oven racks so that one is in the center of the oven. Preheat the oven to convection bake at 400°F.

2. Make the pastry and roll out half of it to line a 9-inch pie pan.

3. In a large bowl, toss the apples with the sugar, flour, cinnamon, nutmeg, if using, and salt. Put the apple mixture into the pan and dot with the butter.

4. Roll out the remaining pastry into a round to fit the top of the pie. Place over the apples.

(continued)

Moisten the edges and turn them under. Crimp them to seal. With the tip of a knife or a fork, cut vent holes in several places in the top crust. Brush the pastry with milk and sprinkle with sugar or cinnamon sugar if desired.

5. Bake the pie in the center of the oven for 35 to 45 minutes or until the crust is nicely browned and the apples are tender. Cool on a rack.

Dutch Apple Pie

Before baking, cut large vents in the top crust and omit the butter. Five to 10 minutes before the baking time is up, remove the pie from the oven and pour $1/2$ cup heavy cream into the pie through the vents. Return the pie to the oven and finish baking.

Apple-Rhubarb Pie

Increase the sugar to 1 cup and replace half the apples with sliced fresh rhubarb. Bake as directed above.

Cinnamon Candy Apple Pie

Omit the cinnamon and nutmeg and add 3 tablespoons red cinnamon candies to the sugar. Cut the top crust pastry into strips and weave a lattice crust on the top. Bake as directed above.

Apple-Raisin Pie

Add $1/2$ cup seedless golden or dark raisins to the apples.

Streusel Apple Pie

Omit the top crust and the butter. Top the pie with a mixture of $1/4$ cup packed light or dark brown sugar, $1/2$ cup all-purpose flour, and 4 tablespoons butter, blended to make moist crumbs.

Holiday Pumpkin Pie

$^3/_4$ cup packed light or dark brown sugar

$^1/_2$ teaspoon salt

$1^1/_2$ tablespoons pumpkin pie spice

2 eggs

2 cups or one 15-ounce can plain pumpkin puree

$1^1/_2$ cups heavy cream, half-and-half, or undiluted
    evaporated milk

Half recipe Flaky Pastry (page 37)

1. Position the oven racks so that one rack is in the center of the oven. Preheat the oven to convection bake at 350°F.

2. Make the pastry and roll it out to line a 9-inch pie pan.

3. Measure the brown sugar, salt, pie spice, eggs, pumpkin, and cream into a large bowl. With a whisk, stir all the ingredients together until smooth and well blended.

4. Pour the pumpkin mixture into the pie shell. Place the pie into the center of the oven and bake for 35 to 45 minutes, until the pie tests done (see headnote). Remove the pie from the oven and cool on a wire rack. Chill before serving, if desired.

Pumpkin pie is a custard-type pie that bakes most easily in the convection oven at a steady temperature. Because ovens can vary, if your pie gets too dark too soon, reduce the oven temperature by another 25 degrees. The pie is done when a knife inserted just off center comes out clean and the center of the pie still jiggles but is not liquid. This will be in 10 to 15 minutes less time than if baked in a conventional oven. I prefer pumpkin pie chilled rather than hot from the oven, which allows me to bake it a day in advance.

■ Makes one 9-inch pie

Cranberry-Raisin Lattice-Top Pie

Flaky Pastry (page 37)

3 cups cranberries, fresh or thawed

2 tablespoons all-purpose flour

2 cups sugar, plus 1 tablespoon for the top of the
    pie

$^1/_4$ teaspoon salt

1 cup golden raisins

$^2/_3$ cup boiling water

2 teaspoons freshly grated lemon or orange zest

2 tablespoons butter

1 cup slivered almonds, toasted

1 egg, beaten

1. On a lightly floured surface, roll out half the pastry to make an 11-inch circle. Transfer to a 9-inch pie pan; trim and refrigerate until ready to use along with the remaining pastry.

2. Combine the cranberries, flour, 2 cups of the sugar, the salt, water, raisins, and lemon zest in a saucepan and heat to a boil. Simmer, covered, over medium heat for about 10 minutes, until the cranberries start to pop. Remove from the heat. Add butter. Cool completely.

3. Position the oven racks so that one rack is in the center of the oven. Preheat the oven to convection bake at 375°F.

4. Roll out the second half of the pastry to make an 11-inch circle. With a pastry wheel, cut into eight $^1/_2$-inch strips.

5. Put the fruit filling into the pie shell and sprinkle with the almonds. Moisten the edge of the shell slightly with cold water. Arrange 4 pastry strips 1 inch apart across the filling; press the ends into the rim of the pastry. Place 4 pastry strips across the first ones at right angles to make a lattice. Press the ends to the rim of the pie and crimp. Lightly brush the pastry with the beaten egg and sprinkle with the remaining 1 tablespoon sugar. Bake for 35 to 45 minutes or until the crust is nicely browned. Cool the pie on a wire rack.

Perfect for autumn holiday meals, this pie is best served warm with a scoop of vanilla ice cream. ■ Makes one 9-inch pie

This classic dessert is a "soft-hard" meringue that needs to dry in the oven rather than actually bake. If it is at all browned, the result is a chewy, not delicate base for fresh strawberries or other soft fruits and berries. The convection oven produces an ideally tender meringue that can be made ahead and stored in an airtight container in a cool place for at least 2 weeks. ■ Makes 8 servings

Pavlova

Flour for the baking sheet

4 egg whites (^{1}/2 cup) at room temperature

^{1}/4 teaspoon salt

1 cup sugar

4 teaspoons cornstarch

^{1}/2 teaspoon cream of tartar

1 teaspoon vanilla extract

Sliced fresh strawberries, peaches, black berries, or raspberries and whipped cream for serving

1. Position the oven racks so that one rack is in the center of the oven. Preheat the oven to convection bake at 175°F. Cover a baking sheet with parchment paper and sprinkle evenly with flour. Draw an 8-inch circle in the flour.

2. Combine the egg whites and salt in the large bowl of an electric mixer. Beat at low speed until foamy. Stir the sugar and cornstarch together in a small bowl.

3. Add the cream of tartar and vanilla to the egg whites and increase the speed to high, scraping the bowl once or twice. Add the sugar/cornstarch mixture a heaping tablespoon at a time and continue beating at high speed for at least 8 to 10 minutes, until very stiff.

4. Remove the beaters and with a rubber spatula scoop the meringue into a big pile in the center of the 8-inch circle. With a metal spatula, gently ease the mass into a cake 1^1/2 to 2 inches high. Smooth the edges and top so that it resembles a layer of white cake.

5. Dry in the oven for 5 hours, until the meringue is firm and very light when picked up. If you are serving it right away, top with the fruit and whipped cream. Otherwise, wrap it airtight in a plastic zip-top bag or a tight tin and store in a cool place until you are ready to serve it.

Roasted Fruit Desserts

Roasted fruits take on a rich, concentrated flavor. I love to roast fruits not only for dessert but for breakfast or brunch as well. Apples, bananas, pears, peaches, nectarines, and plums are among the ingredients for these rustic, easy desserts. Many of them can be roasting in the oven while you are enjoying dinner.

Apple Crisp

1 cup packed brown sugar

1 cup all-purpose flour

2 teaspoons ground cinnamon

8 tablespoons (1 stick) cold butter

6 Golden Delicious apples (about 2 pounds),
     peeled, cored, and sliced thin

2 teaspoons freshly squeezed lemon juice

1 teaspoon freshly grated lemon zest

1. Position the oven racks so that there is one rack in the center of the oven. Preheat the oven to convection bake at 350°F. Butter a 9- or 10-inch pie pan or a 9-inch square baking pan.

2. In a small bowl, or in the bowl of a food processor fitted with the steel blade, combine the sugar, flour, and 1 teaspoon of the cinnamon. Slice the butter into the flour mixture and with a pastry blender, or using 10 on-off pulses of the food processor, cut in the butter until the mixture is crumbly.

3. Sprinkle the apples with the remaining 1 teaspoon cinnamon, the lemon juice, and the lemon zest. Arrange the slices in the baking pan. Sprinkle the crumb mixture evenly over the top.

4. Bake in the center of the oven, uncovered, for 35 to 45 minutes or until the apples are fork-tender and the crust is browned and crisp.

Pear Crisp

Use 6 Bartlett or Bosc pears. Replace the cinnamon with $1/2$ teaspoon ground nutmeg.

Peach and Blueberry Crisp

Use 5 large peeled peaches and 1 cup fresh blueberries. Bake for 25 to 30 minutes or until the crust is browned and crisp.

This old-time dessert is still a favorite today. It's really a streusel apple pie baked without a crust.

■ Makes 6 servings

Sometimes it's a case of "the simpler the better." Here, you bake apples in a rich, buttery caramel sauce and it doesn't take much time to get it all together, either. ■ Makes 4 servings

Baked Caramel Apples

4 large Golden Delicious apples, cored

1 cup sugar

8 tablespoons (1 stick) butter

1. Position the oven racks so that one rack is in the center of the oven. Preheat the oven to convection bake at 375°F. Lightly butter a baking dish just large enough to hold the fruit.

2. Peel the bottom half of each apple.

3. Heat the sugar in a heavy skillet over high heat, stirring, until it begins to melt around the edges, about 5 minutes. Reduce the heat to medium and stir until all the sugar is dissolved and the mixture turns a light caramel color.

4. With a whisk, stir in the butter until the butter is melted into the sugar. Cook over medium heat, stirring, until the sauce is smooth.

5. Pour the sauce into the baking dish to cover the bottom. Put the apples in the baking dish with the peeled side down and pour the caramel into the hollowed-out centers. Cover the remainder of the apples with caramel sauce.

6. Bake in the center of the oven for 30 minutes. Using a pair of tongs or two spoons, gently turn the apples over and continue baking, basting two or three times, until the apples are tender, about 15 more minutes.

7. Cool and serve the apples with the sauce spooned over them.

Baked Pears

Wash firm Bosc pears; do not core them, but trim the bottoms of each so they will stand up in the baking dish. Continue with the recipe from step 3.

Cooked bananas are a relative rarity, the New Orleans classic Bananas Foster being one exception. The caramel sauce is simple to make by just boiling the sugar and the sauce can be made hours in advance. The bananas are best served hot from the oven. If macadamia nuts are a bit rich for you, just leave them out, although they are a great embellishment.

■ Makes 4 servings

Roasted Bananas with Macadamia Nuts and Caramel Sauce

1/2 cup sugar

1/2 cup heavy cream

1 to 2 tablespoons dark rum

4 firm but ripe bananas

1/4 cup chopped, toasted macadamia nuts
   (see Note)

1. Position the oven racks so that they are evenly spaced with one rack in the center. Preheat the oven to convection roast at 475°F.

2. For the caramel sauce, bring the sugar and cream to a boil in a heavy saucepan. Boil for 5 minutes, stirring constantly, until the sauce thickens slightly. Remove from the heat and stir in the rum.

3. Arrange the bananas in a buttered, shallow baking dish. Pour the caramel sauce over them and turn to coat. Roast in the center of the oven for 6 to 10 minutes, until heated through. Sprinkle with the nuts. Spoon the caramel sauce over each serving.

Note: To toast macadamia nuts, spread them on a cookie sheet and roast for 3 to 5 minutes at 450°F, until lightly browned. Watch them carefully, as macadamias are oily and toast quickly.

Roasted Peaches with Brown Sugar and Cream

4 ripe peaches, halved and pitted
8 teaspoons butter (1 stick), plus butter for the
    dishes
$^1/_2$ cup packed light brown sugar
4 tablespoons dark rum, optional
Heavy cream

1. Position the oven racks so that one of the racks is in the center of the oven. Preheat the oven to convection roast at 500°F. Butter four individual ovenproof baking dishes.

2. Place two peach halves into each baking dish, cut side up. Place 1 teaspoon butter in the cavity of each peach half. Then spoon 1 tablespoon brown sugar in each.

3. Bake in the center of the oven for 10 minutes, until the edges of the peaches begin to brown and the sugar and butter are bubbly. Remove from the oven.

4. If desired, pour about 1 tablespoon dark rum over each serving and ignite carefully. Serve with heavy cream.

When fresh peaches are in season and ripe, this is a wonderful way to serve them. ■ Makes 4 servings

Roasted Pineapple with Lime and Brown Sugar

1 large, fresh, extrasweet pineapple

2 tablespoons butter, melted

1/2 teaspoon salt

4 tablespoons light or dark brown sugar

2 fresh limes, quartered

6 scoops vanilla ice cream

This is best served warm, a scoop of ice cream melting over each serving. You can get the pineapple ready for roasting and pop it into the oven about 15 minutes before you plan to serve dessert.

■ Makes 6 servings

1. Position the oven racks so that they are evenly spaced, with one rack in the center. Preheat the oven to convection roast at 425°F. Cover a rimless baking sheet with foil and coat with non-stick spray.

2. Slice the top and bottom off the pineapple, cut off the prickly brown skin, and cut out the core. Cut the flesh crosswise into six 1-inch slices.

3. Place the pineapple on the baking sheet, brush with the melted butter, and sprinkle with the salt and brown sugar. Roast for 10 minutes; turn over and roast for 3 to 5 more minutes, until the pineapple is lightly browned on both sides. Place on individual serving dishes and squeeze lime juice over each slice. Top with a scoop of vanilla ice cream and serve immediately.

Index

fudgy walnut brownies, 225

mocha-flavored apple cake with maple caramel frosting, 200–201

oatmeal nut cookies, 222

orange cranberry bread, 194

orange walnut cake, 205

roasted onion, rosemary, and blue cheese pizza, 25

walnut-fig loaf, 162

Wheat berries

slow-roasted four-grain salad, 154

White chocolate

praline-filled chocolate drizzle cookies, 217

white chocolate chip macadamia cookies, 221

Whole-grain breads

about convection baking, 157, 159, 173

cinnamon-raisin bread with walnuts, 170

farmer rye bread, 174–175

honey whole wheat bread, 169

Scandinavian-style pumpernickel, 176

Swedish rye bread, 168

Whole wheat

banana nut bread, 193

cinnamon-raisin bread with walnuts, 170

honey whole wheat bread, 169

in Scandinavian-style pumpernickel, 176

whole wheat muffins, 187

See also Wheat berries

Wild rice

Cornish hens with wild rice-cranberry stuffing and jalapeño jelly glaze, 111–112

slow-roasted four-grain salad, 154

Wine-marinated chicken, 97

Winter squash. See Squash

Winter vegetables, maple-roasted, 133

See also Root vegetables; specific vegetables

Y

Yams

sweet potato, red garnet, and yam salad, 155

yams roasted with orange, 145

Yeast breads. See Breads

Yogurt

tandoori salmon with cucumber yogurt sauce, 124–125

Z

Zucchini

pasta salad with roasted vegetables and feta, 150

primavera pizza, 25

roasted eggplant, zucchini, and red pepper soup, 52

roasted eggplant and zucchini sauce for pasta, 34

roasted ratatouille, 138

roasted vegetable pizza, 25

ABOUT THE AUTHOR

Beatrice Ojakangas is the author of twenty-five cookbooks, and has written for *Bon Appétit, Gourmet, Woman's Day, Family Circle, Redbook, Cooking Light,* and *Ladies' Home Journal,* among other publications. She has appeared on the Food Network, *Martha Stewart Living,* and *Baking with Julia,* and teaches cooking classes across the country. She lives in Minnesota.